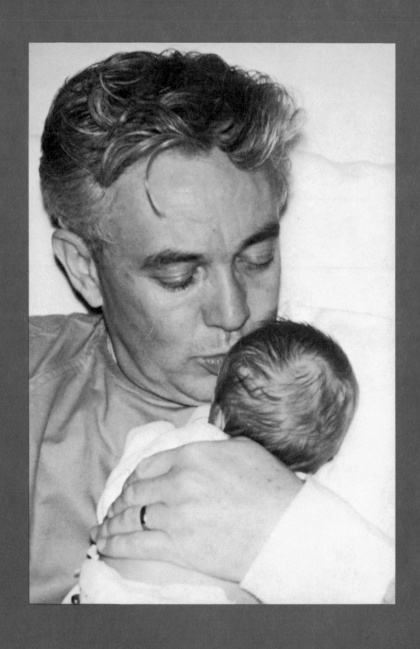

Krinkle Nose

By the same author:
Commitment to Care
Lonely God, Lonely Man
The Autonomous Man
The Einstein Myth
The Ives Papers [*Ed.*]

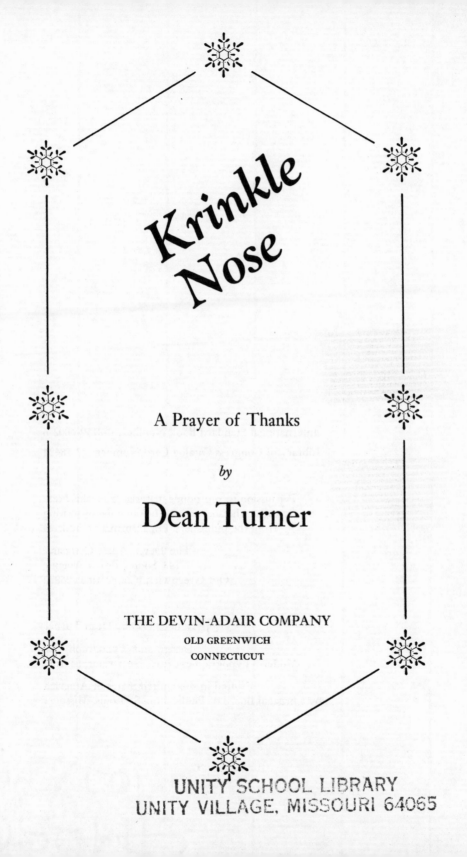

Krinkle Nose

A Prayer of Thanks

by

Dean Turner

THE DEVIN-ADAIR COMPANY
OLD GREENWICH
CONNECTICUT

International Standard Book Number: 0-8159-6002-6

Library of Congress Catalog Card Number: 77-78424

The Devin-Adair Company
143 Sound Beach Avenue
Old Greenwich, Connecticut 06870

Design and Typography by
Modern Typographers, Inc., Clearwater, Florida

Printed in the United States of America
by Christian Board of Publication, St. Louis, Missouri

For my daughter

SUMMER

(born after this book was written)

Know that whatever becomes of us in time,
whatever you do, whatever might befall you,
we will always love you, Our Little Girl.

Let your father and mother have joy;
let her who bore you exult.

Proverbs 23:25

I.

ord, I remember that night my little son was born. His mother had been in labor for fourteen hours. Nancy-bo awoke at two o'clock that Wednesday morning (October 11, 1972) in biting pains. At five o'clock we entered the hospital, certain that this was the day because all of the symptoms conformed to the classic description of that awe-striking process that normally brings a baby into the world. At thirty minutes past noon they wheeled my woman into the delivery room only to conclude, in time, that she should be returned to her quarters.

There I stood beside Nancy holding her, kissing her, letting her grasp me and tightly cling to my hands as the pains mounted over and over. Soon the afternoon hours turned into sheer torture as the little baby strove to come out, but could not, for my woman's muscles around his head were so tight the best drugs designed to relax and dilate them would not work. Dr. Wayne Livermore—sensitive, dedicated, very careful obstetrician—worked with Nancy-bo until six thirty that evening, until it was no longer safe to strive for a natural birth.

No woman could ever possibly be more cooperative with her doctor in trying to deliver her child. Nancy made perfectly coordinated efforts to push our little baby into the world, and it was obvious that he wanted out. I could see the top of his head, that he had a lot of hair, that he was trying to come into the world. Nancy breathed exactly as she had trained herself to breathe, to expedite the delivery, to minimize the pain. She exerted her whole being, made total efforts to thrust our little baby through the natural gate to life. But it would not work. Dr. Livermore wanted to give it every chance, short of going too far.

I wanted to be present to see my child born and to comfort my wife. At the peaks of her pain I talked to her about every imaginable kind of childish thing, to take her mind off of the pain, to alleviate it as much as I could. I talked to her because she asked me to talk to her. She wanted me to be present, to see our little baby born. Besides, I wanted to be there to share in it, to be as much a part of it as possible. The labor pains struck sharper and sharper, Nancy gripped me harder and harder, and I talked to her during each of these convolutions of torment.

"Ten little lambs went running away; one said to the others, I'm going to stay, for I love my mama and I love my daddy, but they're telling me now: Make your own paddy!"

Somehow, I managed to contrive innumerable verses (no few of which undoubtedly were quite corny and silly) as that weary afternoon eventually wore my woman to the point of exhaustion. Dr. Livermore repeatedly checked Nancy's vital signs, to give natural birth every chance short of real danger. I watched my woman lying there totally drained, her whole body covered with tiny beads of cold perspiration. I was growing impatient and worried. It had become obvious to me that our little baby could not come out. The dilation had not increased for hours. Then finally, at six thirty, Dr. Livermore said, "We'll have to do a

Caesarean, Nancy. Your dilation isn't adequate. We don't want to take real risks. You couldn't have tried harder or cooperated better. But now everything will be all right."

They wheeled her into the surgery room, which is where my permission to be present had to stop. There, two skillful surgeons took out our baby by a precise and flawless operation that was quick and right. Dr. Livermore cut a smooth and proper cross-section low over Nancy's abdomen—a line curved like the edge of a quarter moon, low enough that it would not show if my woman ever wanted to swim in a bikini style bathing suit. Safely they lifted my baby out of his mother's womb; they cut his umbilical cord, and thanks to Drs. Wayne Livermore and Fred Roukema, at 6:59 he breathed his first breath of life in this world.

Our pediatrician was Dr. Donald Cook. This gentle, cheerful man wheeled our little baby out in a bassinette, where I was waiting just this side of the surgery-hall entrance doors. A smile beamed on his face as he approached me. I looked at our tiny baby asleep in his basket. However imaginative a man is, it is impossible for him to have a clear advance image of what his baby will look like when it comes. I was unspeakably well pleased. His little head was noticeably shaped like mine. His face had a true baby handsomeness. His head was clean, with beautiful pink skin, with none of the bruises, marks, or mis-shapen effects caused by the trauma of struggling through life's natural gate.

Dr. Cook exulted.

"You are the father of a healthy, normal, vigorous little seven pound son! To be exact, he weighs six pounds and fourteen ounces. I've checked him thoroughly, and as far as we can tell, everything about him is natural and perfect. His mother is quite all right. Everything went well."

Dear Lord, thank you. Thank you for little Taos, my son. Thank you, that his beautiful mother is alive and well.

3

I remember how she used occasionally to moan in her sleep, as she dreamed that he might be born with club feet, which is a gene that runs somewhere in the family and sometimes strikes. But we know that such things come from chemical accidents, not from any express will of yours that some of your children be born less fortunate than others. If our little son had been born less fortunate, we would still love him the same, and Lord, we would love you no less.

Thank you for Taos Lee, our son, our soft and beautiful little baby boy.

II.

Dear Lord, I thank you that my wife and little son are now together in that hospital room. I promised you that if you would bring me a healthy, normal little child, and if you would bring Nancy out of that surgery room well and safe, then I would devote the rest of my life to doing your will. In doing that, was I playing a game with you, Lord, that no one has a right to play? Shouldn't I devote myself to serving you anyway, no matter what misfortunes might rise on the road of my life? If little Taos had been stillborn, or born abnormal; or, if we had lost his mother when he was born, should I then love you or be devoted to your service any the less? I know the answers to these questions, Lord, without your having to tell them to me; nonetheless, I'm glad that you indulge us in our little games, although I'm sure it must sometimes pain you very much when we overdo them or when they get really out of hand.

Nancy-bo lay in the intensive care room last night until early hours in the morning. I stayed with her for only a few minutes. Dr. Livermore said, "It's best that Nancy be by herself in here, without anyone around who might communicate germs. She'll be all right. I think you should get

5

some sleep yourself and come back tomorrow." Whereupon, I drove home and proceeded to call everyone concerned on both sides of our family, plus hosts of friends—to announce this singularly jubilant news.

At about midnight Nancy came out of her anesthesia to find herself alone in the recovery room, groggy, wondering if her little baby had been taken out of her alive. After she was wheeled to her room she managed to dial and connect with me after considerable strain. "Dean Dean," she spoke effortfully, "What happened? Is my little baby all right? Is it alive? Is it a little boy? A little girl?"

"You are the proud mother of an unspeakably beautiful little seven pound son. He is normal and strong. He doesn't look like babies who are natural born. He came out very clean. No marks, abrasions on his head, nor anything like that. He's perfect! He's such a handsome little fellow! He has my head, of course, and your blue eyes and skin. I've called the whole world. Everybody knows we have a little son. Your father was elated. I've never heard him so glad about anything. Our Texas friends Millie and Al went to tell Grannie [my little mother]—I wish she had a phone! I also called Judy and Gordy."

By noon today Nancy's maternity room was inundated with flowers. There was a wicker baby carriage with yellow daisies and baby's breath. There was a china red wagon with baby carnations in colors galore. Also a china baby block on wheels with roses. A china baby lamb with an opulence of tiny colored flowers. There were potted plants, and an earthenware kitty kat with straw flowers and wings of angels. I had to carry them home in two trips to make room for all the new ones coming in.

Needless to say, Taos takes after his Daddy (i.e., in his good nature and good looks) and in the fact that he never cries—except when he feels like it.

6

He is taking his mother's milk now, Lord. What a ravenous appetite he has, and what a divine sight he and his mother are. His mother looks infinitely like a mother should, putting his little head and mouth to her beautiful breast, where happily his milk comes easily and fully—after only a minimum of sometimes frustrating suckling to start it to flow.

I feel a little uneasy holding him, Lord. He is almost disturbingly tender. He seems so fragile, so dependent and helpless. I've never held a baby before, except on occasions when it was someone else's, which I now realize is entirely a different thing. For this little boy is our son, a new little person born of our seed, our hope, our purpose. I love for him to sleep on my shoulder, where I can feel his sweet breath touch my face. I love to hold him secure in my arms.

This afternoon they took and developed his pictures, which are truly well done. Taos looks exactly like himself. His left eye appears to have some character of its own—if you don't mind a euphemism expressing the fact that it seems slightly crooked. But then, one would conclude from looking at them in their little baskets in the show window, that newborn's faces simply never come out perfectly symmetrical. Taos's right lid seems to fall slightly lower over its eye than does the left one, as though he were skeptically pondering the plausibility or veracity of something I had just told him.

Thank you, Dear God, for the joy of his name. Nancy and I passed into that little town in New Mexico one afternoon to visit. Then driving away we chanced upon the Rio Grande River, where one standing on the bridge can see hundreds of feet below him only by staring straight down a sheer, overwhelming precipice. Neither of us had ever seen a more awesome sight in America. A deluge had passed that morning leaving two rainbows straddling the canyon—

a saturnalia of colors such as we had never before seen. Whence out of the blue, my woman said, "If we ever have a little baby and he is a boy, then I want to name him *Taos*."

Maybe a moment passed before I responded to that. But it was not because I needed to ponder the logic in my woman's motivation behind this sudden decision—in fact, I learned long ago never to do such a thing. For my wife is the quintessence of Woman, and in the entelechy of her being there is generally a pristine insight into the beautiful, the true, and the good, such as a man can never find in those inferential processes of reasoning he learns about in taking formal courses in logic.

"So be it," I said.

Then I saw a vague image of a little blue eyed, blond boy.

"If and when he comes to us, little woman, we will name him Taos. And I further add, Taos *Lee*, after his granddad, who I am sorry to say is no longer around to see him."

III.

Thank you, God, for the blessing of true friends. I realize the vastness of my good fortune. Also, I know how many human beings feel lonely and cold in their dark world because there is no one around them who cares. Nancy is now home with our little baby, but during her seven days of confinement in the hospital I was not really alone in this house. Our many friends let me pass no evening without either bringing a meal to me or inviting me to dine in their homes. I do not take lightly this good fortune, that there are those who care deeply for us and show it with their actions.

I changed little Taos's bottom today for the first time. His diaper indicated that he had already completely drained himself and needed only to be dried. But now Lord, would not you yourself be taken aback if you were changing a son of your own and he suddenly squirted straight into your eye, then proceeded to soak the wall? I'm sure your own son, the little God-boy Jesus, must have at least once tinkled on Mary and Joseph, after which they surely loved him all the more. Of one thing I am certain, despite the scriptural allusions to her purity, Mary could never really have loved baby Jesus anymore than my woman loves her little son.

9

Now realize I don't mean this blasphemously, Lord. Rather, I mean it gratefully, to tell you how much love and beauty I see in my wife's care for our little boy. It is inconceivable to me that any mother, even the mother of Jesus, could ever see more natural beauty and splendor in her infant baby than Nancy sees in little Taos.

The first day they brought him to her in the hospital, Nancy had held him in her arms for only a few minutes when she said, "Dean Dean, I have only just met little Taos, but already I love him with my whole being."

Of course, Nancy loved Taos while she was carrying him, but not really as Taos. For indeed how could she, when she did not even know who or what he was, except as a little unseen foetus, which she hoped and prayed would some day come out as a little living person. Boy or girl—neither of us could see what "it" would be, except that we longed for either, and knew that we would be happy with whichever it turned out to be.

I used to put my ear to Nancy's big tummy and listen to his little heart beat—putta putta putta putta. Then I would try to imagine what it was inside, and what it would be like at birth. But a man cannot see the splendor of his baby son until he is there as a son to be seen. Taos now has become fully real. He is the actualization of what up and until just recently was in our minds only the *hope* that a possibility for so good a thing would somehow be transformed into the concrete reality of a new little person. Now we can see and touch Taos, hear him, and indeed taste and smell the natural fragrance and sweetness of his skin as a baby *boy*.

Speaking of hearing him, Lord—would that I had the poetry to express the mesmeric music of the sounds he makes in his sleep. The very sound of his breathing somehow conveys to his mother and me a divine innocence, a tenderness that is angelic. His breathing is free from that spiritual discipline, that strain which inevitably inhibits the naturalness of an adult person's style of breathing in his sleep. Something about his breathing—the sounds he makes in being his utter natural self—has the effect of melting me, of relaxing me more than it is normal for a grown human being to relax. I am at a loss of words to describe these sounds, for they are so rare. The least I can say is, they are preciously sweet. I hear in them the harmony of divine naturalness. Nowhere among humans have I ever heard more tranquilizing sounds. I have heard no utterances from any mouth more mellow and mild.

I credit this to you, Lord. But now, let me in passing also credit you for having endowed my son with such powerful lungs. When he cries, surely the neighbors can hear him all the way up this avenue to the edges of Greeley. And I thank you, dearly, for having blessed me with eardrums that do not break even under the onslaught of my son's unrivaled oral power to express his discontentments in life effectively.

Dr. Cook said that Taos should cry at least two hours a day. For this is the only way that he can get the exercise he needs, plus the fact that it is his only way of making his presence felt in the world. Not to mention that his capacity to express himself is so great that he obviously gets frightened by the loudness of his own performance.

My little boy's movements seem incredibly random. His hands jerk tensely back and forth and in all directions. His limbs seem uncontrolled; he kicks, thrashes, and strikes out totally *ad libitum*. And I would not dare to take his hand to try to restrict his motion, for he would rebel against it with all the power of his being; which proves, his movements are not really merely random after all. For obviously, little Taos is a free agent who cherishes his liberty, and his spirit clearly is the ultimate motivating force behind even

11

the seemingly purely random movements of his body. However many random chemical reactions there might be within it, my son's body is strikingly charged with his spirit. Little Taos is a *person*. He is not just an amorphous glob of accidental chemical reactions such as some philosophical vulgarians would have us believe.

My son does everything with dedication—including the way he frees his body from the discomfort of accumulated wastes he needs to expel. His mother and I were discussing this today (the efficacy and frequency with which he discharges to maintain his physical well being and comfort in the world), and we figure that at the rate he is using them now, before Taos is potty trained he will use about eight thousand, two hundred and fifty diapers.

Before I met my little son, the idea of so frequently cleaning his bottom was simply disgruntling when I dared to ponder it seriously. But now, Lord, I have just discovered another of those many unexpected ways in which you teach us the power of real love, which otherwise would leave us only with the burden of drudgerous and uncomely things in the world. For each time Taos does his "duties" and I clean his little bottom, I see again how beautiful it is and kiss it because I love everything about him with my whole soul, including that part of him.

IV.

Speaking of good fortune, Lord, little Taos sleeps throughout the night except for nursing. Some of my friends tell me their babies sleep throughout the day, and lie awake and cry all night. We are truly thankful to you for this blessing—though of course we don't believe that you deliberately inflict the opposite on some parents because you dislike them and want them to lose sleep at night. Even so, every blessing in life is something to be grateful for, even those that are fortuitous, and I regard this one as especially worthy of mentioning. Taos goes to sleep at seven thirty in the evenings, more or less predictably. He awakes only twice for nursing. Otherwise, he sleeps through to about six thirty in the mornings, practically as though he were honoring a contract.

These days Nancy spends much of her time in bed, convalescing from the Caesarean. But it is not in her nature to like lying in bed, and she requires considerable reminding that things will go well while she takes it easy, that she must look out for her health. Taos sleeps in his own little room with trees, birds, butterflies, grass, a cave and a lion that his mother painted on the walls months ago. The lion looks out from the door of his cave. He is life-size and quite life-like, except perhaps he looks more friendly than lions in a natural setting are likely to look when human beings get that close to them.

Thank you for our friends, the Robert Rosses, who gave us their own Molly's crib, which I painted white and blue as soon as little Taos turned out as a boy. It works as well as new; and Lord, I credit the Devil, not you, for the price of a crib when parents have to buy one anew nowdays. It will be a joy to buy new clothes for our little boy, ones that we especially adore and choose. But it is also a joy to receive from our friends so many hand-me-downs that are still strong, colorful, and of great practical use. These days it costs a fortune to buy baby clothes. Now we have a fortune, a vast fortune indeed, in the love of our families and friends—but a financial fortune we have not. To some it might seem a little thing, the three months diaper service gift from the Grandparents Roche. But thank you, Lord, for that very thoughtful and helpful gift, which was a gesture of very real and practical love.

Several times a night I get up to check on Taos. There is no objective need for this, since his mother checks on him and changes his diapers often. But it is a longing in my soul to several times a night just tiptoe in and look at my son lying there in his total dependence and trust in his mother's and father's care. I see in him something that in my most creative imagination I could never see until he actually came into the world. I think in some sense I am now revising my whole concept of beauty and goodness; or rather, the power of this little boy's presence is unmistakably working within me to bring to fruition a comprehension that has been seeded inside me all along. For example, I feel immensely closer to you, now, God, than I have ever felt before, even though I have always felt that you are close to me because my mother took me on her lap and knee and taught me that you love me; indeed, that you will never, never fail to love us all. But I would be a fool if I did not admit that you have always been closer to me than I've been to you, simply because your care is abidingly benevolent while mine often is self-centered and narrow. I know, ideally, that I am supposed to center my life in you. Also, I know that this is not merely an abstract kind of moral duty that plagues us; rather, it is something that would bring real joy into our lives if I always acted on it seriously.

Do you remember, I promised you while Nancy was in the surgery room that if you would bring her and my child out of there alive then I would strengthen the quality of my life for you the rest of my days. Lord, don't let me forget that promise, even though I know you don't deal in bargaining and contracts with your children. I tell you, this little boy in his overwhelming innocence makes me more conscious than ever of the hallowed beauty of your creative love.

I remember once when I was a boy in Sunday School the teacher quoted a scripture from Matthew (18:1–3) which is attributed to Jesus. One day the disciples came up to Jesus and asked, "Lord, which of us will be greatest in the Kingdom of Heaven?" Whereupon, Jesus called a child over to him and sat the little fellow amongst them saying, "Unless you turn to God from your sins and become like this little child, you will never enter into the Kingdom of Heaven."

Now as you know, Lord, like most scriptures that one had a very limited meaning to me at that time. In fact, you must remember how inordinately skinny I was as a boy, and how I left the church every Sunday at noon with a headache, backache, and tail ache because of inadequate adiposity on my posterior to cushion the effect of those hard pews. Oh Lord, how hard they were! And how im-

15

patient was I—sometimes I wanted to scream, having to sit through the interminable sermons of those long-winded preachers pulpiteering abstrusely on matters always far above my head. And my sisters always sitting there by my sides, never allowing me to fidget, nor to open candy wrappers because the faint noise of tearing paper would abuse the dignity of the church. I thank you for giving me the brains to distinguish between Christianity and churchianity, for in my childhood I truly learned to loathe the church. I am a Christian not because of the church, but in spite of it—albeit, I relish my memories of the great church picnics and feasts with their vast array of delicious meat dishes, fancy cooked vegetables, and hordes of cakes, cobblers, and pies.

Maybe someday parish ministers will learn to provide a religious life more meaningful for children—not to mention for adults. Going to church could be, and should be, a dynamic and uplifting experience. This is the way it is in some churches, especially in those where everyone contributes to an informal worship meeting, and people uninterested in soporific preachers don't have to sit through their longwinded sermons. "Suffer little children"—they, especially, should be spared this negative, anti-inspirational "worship." Lord, any worship of you should be *vital*. It should be spontaneous, and should come from the heart. I have seen it, sometimes, with the Quakers and the Mormons.

That particular scripture now haunts me. It appears in my mind recurrently, and I can attribute it to nought but this tiny baby, this disquietingly helpless little infant who is my son.

I now wonder, What was it Jesus had in his mind that might have prompted him to say such a thing about little children? Why did he say that they are the greatest in the Kingdom of Heaven?

V.

The first time I held him, Lord, I felt uneasy, insecure, awkward. But I realize now that loving parents naturally tend to overestimate the delicacy and fragility of their baby children. How could mankind have survived the ravages of primitive life if babies were as delicate as we generally tend to imagine they are at birth? Before Nancy and Taos came home from the hospital, I had sterilized every room so that this house probably was safer than the hospital itself. The day he left the hospital, Taos had fallen in weight to only six pounds and seven ounces, and he seemed frighteningly wee and weak. Now, they tell me that this loss in weight is normal, especially for newborns feeding strictly on their mother's natural milk. Because of more fat in the milk, babies who are on bottles tend to add more weight. Yet, Taos's feeding from his mother has given him substantially greater real strength, i.e., the kind that more successfully immunizes him to infections and sustains his wherewithal to survive—despite the fact that infants remain skinnier while on their mother's milk.

Nonetheless, it is disconcerting to see my son so thin; and consequently, I'm glad you're there to talk to, Lord, if for no other reason than the fact that when all is said and done you are our only dependable source of security in any event. Even so, you are no security at all if we don't act to save ourselves. Hence, I saw fit to scrub and disinfect every square inch of every wall, floor, piece of furniture in the home, and even the car. The day Taos came home our's probably was the most ascepticized car ever ridden in by man. At any rate, I've never smelt one more sweetly clean with the fragrance of Lysol spray. Our nurse friends had insisted on elaborately disinfecting Taos's environment. Thus in this house now I can't see how the most willful germ could possibly survive. Our friends are thoughtful not to come by to see Taos at this time, until he has taken a hardier hold on life. Dr. Cook insists that he is really quite strong. Yet he is so tiny. He seems so very vulnerable.

I'm sure behind this apprehension about his delicacy is a fear that my son might die. It isn't just that we tried so long before we had him—we were married seven years. Nor is it the fact that Nancy-bo suffered two miscarriages along the way. During her last pregnancy before Taos was conceived, five months had passed, and Nancy-bo was getting big. I remember how proudly I walked beside her in the streets. I knew that people would see that this magnificent young woman was *my* woman, and that this big roundness in her middle portended the coming of *my* child. I am grateful, Lord, for the joy of that hope while it lasted, with its contribution to the meaning of our love—even though one day Nancy didn't feel pregnant any more, and then after two weeks a Doptone test proved that the little foetus she was carrying was dead.

In the hospital they stuck long needles through her belly into her uterus to induce abortion, in order that she wouldn't carry the expired foetus. I remember in the hospital in Denver while they were photographing the foetus with sound I prayed to you begging you to make our little

18

baby be alive. We wanted it like we want air to breathe. We needed it like we need a warm sunrise after a cold night. I prayed and prayed. Then we had to return home, to wait two days to get a report on the test's results. Finally, Nancy learned in Dr. Bechtel's office that the baby was dead. There could be no alternative to removing it from her body, which he did by injecting a saline solution into her uterus. This irritated and incited the muscles to convulse and throw the little thing out.

I have not forgotten the excruciating pain. Nancy insisted that I not be in the hospital room to see her and hear her suffering. Thank you, Lord, for the care of my beautiful mother-in-law, who came from Connecticut to be at her side. But even at the end of the hall at times I could hear my woman groan. My woman can take pain like a Stoic. Her capacity to suffer when she knows she can't escape it is nought less than lofty. Nonetheless, with this kind of pain no woman can do less than occasionally cry out.

Lord, it is obvious that you cannot answer all of our prayers. It is evident that you cannot always intervene to do for us the good things that we would ask you to do. Jesus said, "Ask, and it shall be given to you." I believe that you are at any time doing all the good for your children that you can possibly do, whether we call upon you to do it or not. Yet, I have to believe that it means something to you when we address ourselves directly to you in prayer, even when you can't always respond to our supplications as we would have you do. Lord, it means more to me than I can express, that I am always free and welcome to ask you for something, even knowing that you can't always give me what I seek.

I don't want to lose little Taos. I find that the meaning of my life is now centered in him, just as it is centered in his mother. The meaning of each of us is found in the mean-

19

ing of all of us. Little Taos is my son forever, no less than his mother is my wife, my sweetheart, forever. More than once you have admonished us to have faith—and faith I have. Notwithstanding your charge to believe, I ask you anyway, Lord, to help me to protect my son. Right now he only in the faintest sense realizes that I am his father. He does not respond to me as an end in myself; rather, he just responds instinctively to his own needs, and is only beginning to distinguish between the in-here and the out-there. He has yet even to find his toes, and to separate them in his mind from his self. But it is obvious that Taos is a *spirit*, that he has a mind with which eventually he will distinguish between himself and his daddy, and between his self and his mommy. The individual and his environment are of course separate; existentially and logically they are necessarily distinct. And little Taos already is beginning to vaguely discern this fact. It is evident that he already has awareness of when he does and does not have hold of his mother's breast. Hungry and in need, he reaches *out*; and this reaching out clearly evinces a beginning conception of what is in himself and what is *out there*.

Show me, Lord, how to safeguard this little boy. Don't let me fail to give him whatever warmth and protection he needs to hold onto his life. I want him to grow and live. I want him to find all of the value, meaning, and beauty that is out there in the world you created for him. I want him to know Nancy as his mother, not only as his blanket and his milk. I want him to learn to ache inside as he discovers the abiding beauty of his mother's love. I want him to know me as his daddy, with whom he can wrestle, run, and laugh. I want him to know that his home is his home, not merely a warm place.

Watch after our little baby, when we cannot. Touch him with the grace of your power, insofar as you can.

VI.

Taos is six weeks old now. We've been bathing him for two weeks. Nancy lowers him into the little green plastic tub, which is a third filled with warm water. Of course she is careful not to make the water too warm. Even so, Taos invariably protests uproariously; he kicks and thrashes madly and lets out ear-splitting screams—at first. Apparently, he is discomforted by the sudden change of temperature on his skin, although the water is only tepid. Perhaps he is discomforted by the sudden nakedness, since he cherishes being warm. Maybe he feels threatened a bit by the water, even though it is never higher than his waist. Finally, along the end of the bath he adjusts and seems to get over his misery. But in the process he splashes half the water out on his mother and me, and soaks the wall and the rug.

I would feel very awkward trying to bathe him myself. His mother shows uncanny skill in handling him while cleaning him. In only a couple of minutes she is able to transform him from a miserable to a comfortable little fellow. I believe that these baths are a vital experience. At least they are the first thing that I can recall in my life—my mother bathing me in the kitchen sink when I was between two and three. By no means can I recall any of her words. Yet, I distinctly remember the joyfulness of her talking lovingly to me as she bathed me in the sink.

Taos's bath is a ritual in our family now. The two of us are usually present to bathe him. I place the tub of water on top of his changing stand; thereupon, Nancy proceeds to bathe him gently with a soft rag, while we both cajole him to calm down, then console and praise him. I predict that in time Taos will come to anticipate his ablutions with a special pleasure. It will become a little ritual that is happy and play-ful—similar, for example, to his diaper changing ritual on top of the stand. He used to abhor being changed. Again, I think it was the discomfort of being suddenly unclothed. But now, each time we change him he smiles and responds gleefully to our sweet talk to him, and to our singing and whistling.

"You little *R A S C A L* you! Daddy *loves* you!"

Somehow, calling Taos "rascal" in the unmistakably affectionate tone his presence inspires, conveys to him the fact that I truly love him. It assures him that I am changing him because I *care* for *him*; that, not only am I seeking to clean his bottom (as could any dutiful but unfeeling nurse), but that I love doing it because I love whom I am doing it to. I love to listen when Nancy-bo is performing the same ritual. Taos gurgles and coos. His whole face smiles. The displeasure of being changed is a thing of the past. These frequent meetings on top of the changing table have become a special little get-together which he looks forward to with joy. He believes that we place him on the stand to play with him, to love him, to make him happy. And as a matter of fact, that is precisely what we do. Cleaning his little bottom is actually a secondary matter; for primarily, it is his hap-piness that makes us happy. It is a different thing, indeed, from what I used to imagine changing diapers would be.

VII.

In my lifetime I've never found more to be grateful for than on this Thanksgiving Day. Lord, we are spending the holidays here in Greenwich, Connecticut, with Nancy's family who are seeing Taos for the first time. My sister-in-law's little boy, Jay, is the same age as Taos, but is twice as heavy, and rolls over Taos like a juggernaut. He has a round cherubic face with great beautiful eyes that are just beginning to turn brown. Nancy-bo has affectionately named him Wo-fats. He is a most extraordinary baby boy. Beside my tiny boy he is a giant.

Grandfather Roche just placed Taos and Jay together on the couch as subjects for a picture, leaning them slightly together for mutual support since neither is capable of sitting up on his own. Whereupon, Jay promptly proceeded to roll over on Taos and veritably smashed him!

They may have to operate on little Jay. Like his older brother, he has a club foot and may need recurrent surgery before a maximum correction is accomplished.

Lord, I know that you love little Jay and Billy just as you love Uncle Joe, all of whom were born with this abnormality in their feet. I'm sure that you have reasons for permitting chance mutations in genes that can bring these phy-

23

sical defects into life. In a world where nothing could ever happen by chance, or in which nothing could ever accidentally go wrong, it would seem that human beings as such could not exist at all. It surely is no accident that accidents can happen. Nor is it purely a chance phenomenon that many things can happen by chance. I'm sure that when you created the world you did it in such a way as to guarantee that there would be room in it for the possibility that some things could happen accidentally or by chance.

If we can't love you in a world of risks, Lord, then we can't love you at all.

If we can't endure some suffering because of things challenging us as they do, then we can't stand beside Jesus as he has asked us to do. He faced the ultimate challenge straight in the eye, then set an example of how we must be prepared to suffer for the sake of goodness whenever a situation might demand it.

I'm certain that you are pained as much as little Jay and Billy by their handicap and suffering. Otherwise, you would not possess even the empathy of their parents, who if they had any choice in the matter certainly would have given their children normal feet.

Dear God, this Thanksgiving Day I thank you for all of our blessings, including all the possibilities for a good life for little Jay and Billy—who, though encumbered by clubbed feet, are preciously beautiful and are a tribute to your creative love. I like to run and play with Billy. He is four. This morning we played football on the front yard grass, where he stained the knees of his new dress suit green —which I'm not at all certain can be cleaned—Lord, don't tell his mother!

24

VIII.

Before my marriage and the coming of Taos, it is curious how poorly I understood the value of rituals. I used to look down my nose at any kind of ritualistic approach to conducting the affairs of life. And there is no doubt in my mind that this is due to a negative emotional reaction to adult church rituals which I found to be mechanical and empty, for me as a captive-audience child. Now, however, I am convinced that life's most meaningful and valuable experiences are found in participating in little rituals that grow out of the beauties discovered in personal love.

For example, Taos falls asleep on my chest and shoulder every night as I lie on the beanbag chair. His little head lies next to mine, and I can marvel at the beauteous repose in his face. I can listen keenly to the sounds he makes in his sleep and feel the sweet miracle of his breath of life. He places his clasped hand just under my chin, where I can wonder at the delicacy of its design. I hold my hand gently over his back and feel him breathe. I feel the fascination of his goodness—that it is infinitely better for him to be alive, and be my son, than for him not to exist at all.

After he falls asleep I could of course take him up to his crib. But instead, I find nothing more joyful than to just continue to lie there holding the wonder of my little boy to my heart.

Sometimes, Taos awakes as I take him up to his crib. When this happens, either his mother or I rock him gently to and fro, while together we sing him a little song:

"It's time to go to bed, go to bed, go to bed,
Oh little boy, our pride and joy.
It's time to go to sleep, go to sleep, go to sleep,
Oh little son, our precious one."

As he falls asleep we lay him in his crib, and pray:

"Now I lay me down to sleep,
I pray the Lord my soul to keep,
Guard me through the starry night,
And bring me safe to morning's light
In mommy's and daddy's loving arms.
Amen."

My favorite afternoon ritual is exercising Taos physically. He sits on my lap on the sofa and I raise him on his legs thirty to forty times. I raise him partially by pulling him up by his arms, while he partially raises himself by using the muscles in his arms and legs. Not only does this keep his muscles strong and in good tone, but he distinctly enjoys it as I raise him each time to a different verse, singing:

"Number one, you are my son,
Number two, how I love you,
Number three, come play with me,

Number four, time for one more,
Number five, look how we jive,
Number six, is what Taos picks,
Number seven, we are in heaven!"
And so on, up to thirty or forty times.

Taos especially enjoys the morning and afternoon sways in his Swingomatic—a loan gift from our neighbors, the Stutlers. We wind it up and he swings gently backwards and forwards for several minutes, betraying a unique pleasure in the soothing yet thrilling motion of his seat. Each time it swings it makes a little clicking sound that for Taos seems to be hypnotic. Except that he does not go into a trance, for he usually follows me with his gaze when I am in front of him moving about. I recently discovered that he easily follows the movement of my fingers with his eyes. Thank you Lord, that my little son's coordination and sense perceptions are normal and sharp.

Taos's face is no longer that of a newborn, but rather that of a little boy. The tendency of his right eyelid to fall too low has vanished, and his features now seem perfectly harmonious. His mother and I often carry him with us to shop in the stores. Nancy says that I beam when people stop to remark on his exceeding good looks. I remember how I used to kid with my male friends about their children: "How fortunate that they look like their mother, instead of like their daddy!" And prophetically, they now reciprocate in kind: "How nice that Taos favors his mother. How lucky, he hasn't his father's face!"

Lord, thank you for his splendid features. Taos's eyelashes are strikingly long. His eyebrows will be full and handsomely cast. It is as though he were designed by the angels who, having taken our order, then filled it to meet the specifications of our fondest hopes. I had no conception of what he would look like before he was born. Nor had I any conception of how he would behave. But now it is as though I had gone looking at all of the little babies in the world, assuming that somehow I would recognize the one who belonged to us whenever I found him. And then, this is how it happened: Taos simply saw me coming as I was looking for him, and when he saw that I was looking at him he cried out: "Da dee! Da dee!"

Lord, I thank you for this very special day (23 December 1972). On my lap this afternoon Taos *laughed* for the first time in his life. I know he has been experimenting with making many different kinds of sounds. His mother and I make a note of each one, wishing that we could capture all of them on tape as keepsakes for life. But not since he was born have I heard him express himself so happily as on this day. It was not just a billing, a coo, or some other fun sound. For Taos is not a baby now; he is a little boy, a complete boy, because he laughed the completely hardy and rapturous laugh of a little boy, albeit for only a couple of seconds. And only once. This is a first! Too bad that his mother was out at the store.

I wonder how soon he will laugh again, for his mother to hear.

IX.

Early this morning I happened to awaken at about three o'clock. I found our bedroom mystically lit up as moonbeams were winging through the windowblinds and falling on my woman's face. I lay there marveling at Nancy's splendid features. I know Nancy-bo has twenty-six years now, and she has had no few hard knocks in life. Yet, it is remarkable how she has retained the lineless skin and blooming complexion of an adolescent girl. Looking at her face, I found myself gradually overcome with a deep aching. I was not aching at the thought of how empty my soul would be if for some reason I were to lose her—although, if that were to happen, it certainly would be the most painful trial of my life. Rather, I lay aching because I was trying to absorb all of the beauty that was there in front of me; I wanted to take all of it into myself, secure it, and know that I could conserve all of it within me forever. The aching came from my realization that there was more beauty there than I could ever possibly absorb, that it would be impossible to ever take *all* of it into me, that it would take an eternity of time for me to apprehend all of the beauty and meaning inherent in the being and love of this woman at my side.

I was unable to return to sleep because of my aching. Now, many modern philosophers insist that there are no certain truths and absolute values in this world. But Lord, how dry and insipid their spirits must be if they really mean what they say. I am *certain* that my good fortune in life is so great that it is *absolutely* impossible for me ever to be adequately grateful for it. My woman is The One Woman, the only woman, who could ever set my heart on fire, and then sustain that fire forever just by continuing to be the kind of person that she is.

Don't let this suggest that I was a fool for infatuation. Lord, you know that I could never marry any woman only for her physical form—though certainly I see in my wife's body and face the ultimate Beauty of Woman. It is as though the angels made me first, and then, studying my nature and longings exactly as an individual man, proceeded to create Nancy Margaret Roche to match my needs perfectly.

I remember everything as vividly as though it had happened just yesterday. I, a poor Texas school teacher, went to Rye High School in New York for no other reason than to pursue a more lucrative wherewithal to live. That I would find in that high school the Woman for Me never would have occurred to me even once. That I would meet in one of my Spanish classes a sixteen year old girl, then come to deem her the One destined to be My Woman Forever—I, a thirty-six year old man, never would have anticipated any more than I would have anticipated some stranger approaching me in the street and offering me the Presidency of Harvard. But such is life, for those of us whose fortune is so great it creates a warm seizure in us every single day that passes.

In my lifetime I have encountered my share of disserendipities; but Lord, serendipity such as this—finding

Nancy Roche in that high school class—I think the most imaginative dreamer alive could simply never have foreseen. It is not that I never knew basically what I wanted in a woman. Altogether the contrary, I had known this since I was first old enough to imagine that someday I would wish to seek after a wife. It is rather that I knew quite exactly the kind of woman whom I really needed and wanted, and also knew that beyond the ghost of a doubt I would recognize her when our paths happened to cross. Dear God, you know how many women I had dated in my life before I met the Right One (rich and poor, black, yellow, brown, white and red—in twenty different countries); and you know how many times through all those lonely years I had to decide that this one, and that one, were not really the right ones for me at all. Somehow, I knew that I would know when the Woman for Me came along.

Then, there she appeared that first day of classes in Rye High School, sitting in the third row, dressed in a pale blue blouse and blue jumper, *obviously* the most beautiful woman your divine hands could ever create for me. The bell rang, and I watched her walk out of that room, virtually unable to believe what my eyes saw. Lithe limbed, self-consciously graceful, a more radiantly feminine woman than I had ever seen or imagined. Her smart brown hair fell over her face like a morning mist falls over a mountain—which is to say, exactly as it *should* when styled by a natural artist whose sense of beauty is perfectly right. Nancy's hair was obviously done up, yet it had that naturalness about it which gives mere tonsorial mode a true style. Here before my eyes was what I had always fancied essential in a woman—*my* woman—all the days of my life: *irresistible style.*

Yet, our love did not begin logically there. For logically, as a man twenty years her senior I knew that I had to distinguish between the physical genre and the *persona* inside. Albeit, it was the beginning emotionally and spiritually because the spark of the woman I was to love and marry distinctly shone through that flesh lighting up my spirit as it lit up her face. All my life I had been looking for a woman whose insides shone through her outside, or whose outside reflected her inside. I mean a woman whose inner beauty is heralded in what I can see with my eyes, and whose outer beauty reveals what I can touch with my spirit.

We allowed months to pass before we dared to communicate our private thoughts to one another openly. Yet somehow, I knew that she knew that I knew that she knew. In a man and woman who are deeply attracted to each other there is always an unconscious radar that sends little messages between heart and heart.

Of course, the situation was delicate, considering the formal stricture in that school against teachers fraternizing with students. Not to mention the danger of embarrassment for Nancy-bo if I had publicly advertised my feelings for her even inadvertently. Consequently, as the cliché would have it, we had to "play it cool," and be as careful as mice tiptoeing in between sleeping cats. I knew that I was in love with a distinct woman, not a girl, when I discovered the uncanny discretion and judgment she revealed in handling the matter.

As for our first completely open self-disclosure, it began in the hallway on a precious spring day. Through our usual form of communication—our unconscious wireless telegraphy—we had arranged to *just happen* to meet enroute to a class.

"Mr. T., couldn't you help me a little with my Spanish grammar—these subjunctives are taxing my capacity to understand!"

"Surely, Nancita. I'll be in the study hall today after school at three fifteen. I'm sure that with a little help you'll get your subjunctives down pat."

"Then I'll see you there."

Of course, I knew and she knew that it was the grammar of love we had been starved to discuss, which had been reined back for months. That afternoon, we sat close to each other at the end of a study hall table. Within ear shot of other students, we quite seriously discussed problems of Spanish for about five minutes, each of us knowing that in reality we were there to discuss not the conjugation of verbs, but rather, the proper conjugation of our feelings for each other. This was my "first date" with Nancita Roche, the girl my radar now told me unmistakably had been born in this world to become My Woman. I detected about her an ever-so-faint fragrance of Joy, that elegant perfume that complements her as none other can. After minutes, the nearby students departed for home, and we were at last alone; meaning, our selves could now meet free from painful distance. We then talked about everything except Spanish grammar, knowing that it would lead eventually to talking seriously about us.

I shall always remember that first day when we came together alone. I shall remember discovering the vast territory of her fabulous mind, her acute awareness, her sharp wit. It was like longing all my life to sail across the blue ocean, then one sunny day at last setting sail.

I remember touching her hand for the first time, being close to this unsurpassably charming woman, as she sat next to me in her spicy patchwork blouse and tan skirt.

Before that school year ended we met and met, both of us careful, each making certain that we were never generating a situation that we could not handle without trouble.

We both sensed that we were right for each other, that indeed, if our love was not valid and good, then there never was anything on this earth really valid and good. But we let it develop with restraint, style and grace. There was no pushing, no rushing, no pressuring of any kind. I felt overwhelmed by the rare judgment, discernment, and prudence of this complete woman who was only sixteen.

Lord, do you remember the day I sent the students to the blackboard, ostensibly to conjugate verbs in the subjunctive mood? Surely you know our pretexts perfectly, our guises and little games. I must confess, I did it solely in order that I could watch Nancy-bo with chalk in her hand, aching after the sight of her in that red blouse and brown wrap-around skirt. Nobody knew my motives but you and I.

What a blessing was that day.

My woman is a truly belletristic poet. I possess an attaché case with my name inscribed on it by a class of affectionate students in Rye High who gave it to me on my birthday of that year. That black leather case is now filled with poems written by this special girl in my life. Recall, Lord, that afternoon in school when I told Nancy of a treasure I once collected and kept secretly when I was a boy. As you remember, at this point in our relationship we had grown accustomed to exchanging notes in the hallways of that great stone school. On the following day, Nancy furtively slipped a note into my hand as we were passing in the west wing—containing a response to my story of my boyhood treasure:

"In my house, under the stairs,
I've had a box of treasures rare,
Of robins' eggs and smooth round stones,
A green cat's eye, two wishing bones,

34

One bottle cap, a beat-up knife,
Some batteries, an old flashlight,
A white pressed rose, parchment to touch,
A thin gold band, a heart turned dust."

In those hallways, and in passing in the streets, my
woman handed me innumerable poems. And sent some by
mail, for example:

"How can human words express
The volume of my happiness?
How can they speak, when I cannot,
The words for which I've searched and sought?
How can they tell the story of
   the joy, the gift, that is your love?
My words, unlimbered, know not how,
At least not here, at least not now,
To assemble in a line
And form a couplet, form a rhyme,
That would express my lasting pride
To walk, forever, by your side."

That last day of school, I sat alone in the study hall
playing the piano, waiting after classes for Nancy to come.
Finally, she dashed in, jubilantly crying, "By the by, when
did I last tell you that I love you!"

Lord, what sweet gifts time has in store for us when
we dare to believe.

This was little Taos's mother to be.

X.

Lord, how precious is memory, that miraculous endowment which enables us to hold onto things beautiful and conserve their value in our souls. I recall all of the great moments in my life with my woman, back to that first day of school where I felt the beginning of our love. I hold onto such moments as they accumulate, for they are the sustenance of my joy in this life. Yet, I realize now that it is not the "great moments" that over time can sustain our will to live; rather, it is the fact that we have found something intrinsically so good and beautiful that we feel any and every moment spent in its presence is a great moment, even when there is nothing whatever dramatic or sensational going on. This means, simply being in the presence of someone you profoundly love, knowing that you are truly loved in return. When I am with Nancy-bo and Taos—even when we are not attending to one another directly, or not talking to each other—I feel perfectly at home in the world because I feel perfectly at home in their presence. And precisely the converse is true: it is when I am apart from them that I feel least at home in the world and least at home with myself. Apart from them, my feeling of at-homeness in the world rests in my knowledge of the fact that soon I will be with them again.

Thank you, Lord, for the great blessing in my life that I have always felt at home on this earth. It is unmistakably because I was raised in a home where I was always surrounded by love, warmth, and beautiful things. My woman and I are doing for our son what my mother did for me— and what her parents did for her. I know there are many unfortunate children who are raised in an atmosphere of insularity and coldness. Many are made to feel unwanted, un-needed, unappreciated, and unloved. Many are buffeted, rejected, and treated as objects, or only as means to their parents' selfish ends. But I thank you, Lord, that from my infancy to this day my mother always treated me as an end in myself; she always made me feel that I was in and of myself important, meaningful, valuable, and beautiful. My mother made me feel needed, wanted, appreciated, and loved.

I am certain that my capacity to love my wife and son, and others dear to me, was cultivated in me by my mother's love—in that little three room house on a dusty street in Stratford, Texas, where dirt storms could blot out the sun at noon. There was not a paved street within sixty miles. The winds blew dirt as though the Devil were trying to tempt people to despair as he tempted Job. There invariably were more crop failures than successes. And invariably there were few days when the sky was free from dirt and the atmosphere still. Yet, my memory is a treasure house of sacred things that happened to me in that little wind-wailing town.

My mother planted the first trees in Stratford (Chinese elms as hardy as the hills), which still stand today as the pride of her care for forty-seven years. Ruthlessly the elements fought to kill her flowers, fruit trees, and grass. But my mother's spirit dominated the land, and now, her home sits beautiful on that corner which she would never allow to parch. My mother's home, and her presence in it, stands

37

as an ornament to human nobility on that dry and windy plain.

I remember how in the summertime my older brothers and I would play marbles on the dirt yard in front of that house. Now and then I would choose to leave the game, to attend to the more important matter of my mother's love. I would approach the front door of the house and holler through the screen: "Mommy, I love you!" Whereupon my mother, at work at her chores, would holler back: "I love you too, son. I love you the mostest!" But I would not allow for such, so I'd cry in return: "Oh no, I love you the mostest!" And she would insist: "Not so, I love you the mostest!"

Today, my mother is eighty-five. Having borne and cared for nine children, her life has been an endless series of loving self-sacrifices for their happiness and well-being. As far back as my memory reaches, I cannot recall her ever having uttered one word of petty gossip against any human being. She has suffered through truly terrible illnesses, without ever having once complained. Due to polio, her left arm shrank up to an abnormality, and once she lay bedfast with a heart ailment for two years unable to perform any work, which abused her natural style of life. All of this passed during my adolescence, but today I find that hard work is still her chosen style. She never regarded work as a drudgery, not even mopping the floors or washing mountains of dishes. For she never had a lazy streak in her body, nor any disposition in her life to moan or complain. But my mother always deeply cherished play, and her spirit of play makes me glad in my soul to this day. It was from her that I learned the good life consists of a balanced combination of work, love, and play. One must work but love his work. And one must play but love his play. But unless one can work at his love, and play with his love, he will lose the meaning of his love, work, and play. I have heard this preached by more than one, but few are those who can live it as my mother has always lived it.

Lord, I am a teacher and minister. I am conscious of how many of your children suffer from what is called a "crisis of identity." Because in my childhood my home was at all times a spiritual oasis, this problem of identity is something I never experienced at all. Never once have I known the pain of trying to discern who and what I am. Nor have I known the bewilderment of a lack of general principles for making the important decisions in my life. It is not that I have been without my own share of agonies. Nor that I have not had to truck through a wilderness of really trying problems. For I too have been in the streets and alleys of life, where one has to cope with sin, hatred, and terror. You were there watching it, in Mexico City, where seven men with switchblades cut me and my friend almost to bloody meat. You were there in the grade school where my peers made relentless fun of my skinny legs and big buck teeth. "Deany boy has big buck teeth! Deany boy is a kildee bird!" And you were there, when I felt tempted to shoot myself in the foot, fearing I could not handle the terrible responsibilities of my job in the Army.

Etc.

Yet still, I always knew who and what I was. And because of the reality of your love, Lord—which I learned about through my mother's exemplary practice of it in my home—I always had the strength, at the moment of decision, to stay in the arena where the sun shone down on me.

I thank you for my identity. I thank you for my wherewithal to weather the crises of life with my will to live intact. I thank you for my Mother, that very special person, that majestic lady from whom I inherited my life strength, my faith, and my nerve to endure. Today she sits mostly rocking in her rocking chair, in that little rancho red and charcoal ranch house I built for her in her corner in Stratford. White-haired, with very wrinkled pock-marked skin, she is slowly going blind. Yet one still sees that gleam in her eyes, ever-present evidence of her invincible affirmation of life.

Lord, I love my Mother. I love her beautiful wrinkles, her oldness, the indomitable nobility in her labor-worn hands.

To this day she insists that she loves me "the mostest."

And to this day who actually loves who the mostest is an unresolved dispute.

XI.

From birth, little Taos has been raised with music. On his first Valentine's Day his mother and I gave him a party where we gave him a fabulous music box that plays every verse of Rockaby Baby. Taos in turn presented to his mother a charming big box playing "Born Free"— one of Nancy's most favorite songs. I think it could not have been more enchantingly designed. Its sides are colored dark garden green, speckled with little white ells, with white flowers in between the ells. The long box is cream yellow on top and shows angel children flying freely through space. One angel is carrying a little white lamb, plus a magic red-ribboned cane. The other two are carrying a hammock made up of stringed lines of music with black notes—of "Born Free." Lying in the hammock strumming the song with his mandolin is a little boy accompanied by three chirping birds riding the notes.

Of course, Taos cannot write. However, he has his own vocabulary which only his mother and I can understand—the magic language of the heart. Needless to say, he asked me to inscribe a message inside the lid of the music box, saying: "For Mommy, my Favorite Valentine, who loves me, bathes me, nurses me, holds me close, and will always, always hold me in her heart. Taos, 1973."

After cake at the party we played Let's Make Funny Faces and Sounds. Taos then began to laugh exuberantly; he laughed freely, and over and over, as we never knew it was possible for a little boy his age to laugh. I wish that somehow we could have foreseen that it would happen, so that we could have made a recording of his laughter to keep forever. I hope that through his lifetime he will have myriad occasions to laugh. But I cannot imagine him ever laughing more bounteously, or having more genuine fun, than he had on this day.

Taos's collection of music boxes would fill a trunk. If he is still awake when we put him to bed, then he falls asleep listening to the music of one of his boxes. The lamp on his bedroom night stand—a gift from beloved Judy Parker—plays "Frère Jacques," which we accompany by making up rhymes in English to match. Always in his crib are some of his little musical stuffed animals. His blue donkey plays "The Donkey Parade." He loves to pull the string to "Heile Heile, Gansje." He has a rocking chair in the living room—a gift from our neighbors, his godparents, the Swifts. It plays Brahms' "Lullaby."

When I rock Taos in my arms in the living room, he listens with an obviously pleased ear to our very finest classics. Sometimes I play resounding compositions which some might erroneously think would be dramatic only for older persons. But I think little Taos's taste, in fact, might well be more catholic than my own; for he seems disposed to listen to almost anything, even to dirges and cantatas which would lead me to strain. Even for opera he has some ear, which I definitely have not. He likes jazz and ragtime, and especially loves martial music. He shares his mother's ear for the great old songs. He is jubilant when I take him into my arms and prance to college marches. This marching has become a daily affair in the afternoons—which he likes to follow with some yogurt or custard.

Lord, I wish my little boy's life could be just an ever happy song. I wish it could be just an immaculately beautiful symphony, unsullied with dissonance and ugly sounds. I wish that you could spare him the falls, bruises, pains, and disillusionments that lurk in the path of every human being's life. If it were possible, I would ask you to fill his life with the greatest of joys, and nothing but joys. This is the heart of his mother and father speaking who would protect him from all harm. But in our minds we know that this is not possible, that if it were, then you would have made it that way in the beginning. We know that one cannot know the joy of eating until he feels the pain of hunger. This is obvious in little Taos, who always cries before he suckles. Can any man know the joy of reaching out, to unite with a woman in love, until first he has suffered the pain of loneliness, of insufficiency in himself? Who can be anxious to learn, who is not first somehow pained by his ignorance, unsatisfied with it, or less at home in the world because of it? I wish that you could spare our son these pains. But you cannot.

Therefore, Lord, that he may survive these hurts of life with grace, help us to give him every possible encouragement and strength. We know that, in time, he will need to harden his viscera and head; that, along life's road, he would be destroyed if we did not teach him how to stand up and fight. But Lord, we have learned nothing, if we have not learned from Jesus the necessity to keep our hearts soft. I am certain that Jesus was a manly man, who around his tender heart had an armor of great toughness without which he could never have begun to do all that he did for us. But teaching our little boy to *stand* will come in the

43

course of time. For now, help us to treat him to every conceivable form of beauty and warmth, that we may create in his heart a capacity to *feel* those things in life which are sacred, and hence ultimately worth standing for. Let us give him encouragement through access to every kind of beauty—the beauties of nature that are your works of art, the beauty of music, the beauty of clean fun, and above all, the beauty of an absolutely reliant love.

XII.

shall always remember this day (May 19th).

When I chose to be ordained in the Christian ministry, I did it not only to minister to the needs of others, but also to minister to my own. When my son grows up and chooses to take a wife, I shall be uniquely glad to unite him with his woman in a special matrimonial service before God. Indeed let them choose their time and place, and by all means choose their preferred format for a wedding. Assuming, of course, that they would prefer for me to marry them, rather than someone else. If for any reason they were to choose another to perform their marriage, then of course I would honor their choice from the very beginning, imposing myself upon them in no way. But the very thought of it is a distinct joy.

Today, I christened my son.

Lord, is it selfish that I should find in this experience a greater meaning than in any religious service I have ever performed for others?

It has been singularly rewarding to perform the marriages of my very closest friends. How could I forget the Cribellis (two beautiful students who wanted me to marry them because they loved me as I loved them)? I married them before the fireplace in the faculty lounge. Or how could I forget the Staffieris, whom Nancy and I cherish almost as if they were our very own? I married them before the marvelous stained glasses of Temple Buell Chapel—where afternoon sunbeams struck through in breathtaking glory. But Lord, is it not in that inner circle of one's own family that one finds beauty and meaning deeper than he can fi·d it elsewhere in the world? Is not family love the prism through which your grace shines brightest into the world?

Thank you, that I myself should know the exceptional joy of baptizing my own little son.

Should not the ministering of a religious rite always be a joy? And should not it be done in such a way, and by such a person, who can make it most a joy?

Lord, you know that in both the general ministry and the laity many churches put theological formulas of dogma before considerations of real need and beauty. I would not want to needlessly offend my brethren by inviting them to attend the christening of my son. For considering their beliefs affixed to this rite, most of those in my church undoubtedly would regard my ministering it to little Taos at his age as an offense. In my church, Lord, I think sometimes that you are unwelcome because your ways would be incompatible with the ways of the flock. Jesus besought us to live by the spirit, solely by the canons of intrinsic beauty and love. But sometimes we lose sight of this like a man gone blind. Then we bog down in the disputation and propagation of abstract theological and christological dogmas that have little to do with real beauty and love.

I lived a total of twelve years in twenty-one countries. During that time, Lord, I learned that you have children spread at great distances from each other on this earth. Your children have vast differences in their backgrounds and beliefs about you. And generally, people have come by these differences naturally and sincerely. I know that your children have a great variety of ways of loving you. Even within my own church, people live with significant differences in their thinking about you—which I must honor and understand with compassion (while honestly disagreeing) if I am to be a Christian in my heart. Far be it from me to tell *other people* how to structure and conduct their worship services and rites, if they are deriving from their unique approach to you a richer love-relationship with you. I don't want to give my differing brothers unsolicited advice. Nor do I want to make as though *I* am their Heavenly Father, instead of you. I know that you love *all* of your children. All Jews, Moslems, Hindus, Buddhists, Christians, et al. are your children. I know also that you love your children who are atheists or agnostics, though they don't even affirm your existence. But in return for this liberality of spirit, I want freedom to approach you, Lord, with a mind and heart of my own. I want to love you as *I* see fit, with integrity of conscience, with *my* heart, *my* mind, *my* soul. If we aren't free to love you in different ways, then we aren't really *free* to love you at all.

I asked one of my colleagues in the church: "Might I use your chapel to christen my son?" Whereupon, he answered: "Why Sir, your son is only seven months old! Don't you know that before the age of twelve we do not baptize children in our church? Even so, I will convene the elders, and will communicate their decision to you after they have pondered the matter of such an unusual request."

A month later I received the communication of their decision by mail, rejecting the request.

But then, I requested the same of another minister in my church, who replied: "It would indeed be all right for you to christen your son in the chapel of this church." Thus

47

Lord, did I find one of your houses in which to sprinkle my little boy. Amongst the sheep of my fold it is imagined that the *only* "proper" way to baptize a child is by immersion after the age of twelve. Thank you, Lord, that one of my ministerial colleagues could honor *my* belief that the meaning of baptism is the love and beauty that is actually felt therein.

Nancy and I wanted to christen little Taos upon his passing through the threshold of life—which is to say, *now*—not years further down the road. I would not immerse my little boy only seven months old.

But this was no problem, Lord, for we never intended to invite anyone anyway except those exceptional few who have been especially close to Taos. Thus there was no awkwardness for the minister granting us use of his chapel, for no general announcement whatever went out.

When Taos was two months old we bought him a little silver cup, and had inscribed upon it: "Wednesday's child is free from woe." Now this little cup will last for his lifetime, and it will always be his to take wherever he may go. We also bought for Taos a little silver bowl with imprinted leaves around the edges, and shaped like a heart. Last week we had inscribed upon it: "Taos's Baptism: 1/19/73. This is our beloved son in whom we are well pleased." To accompany this little bowl at the christening we bought him a fine, thin silver vase. This morning at eleven o'clock we put a rose in the vase, and placed it and the little heart filled with christening water next to the Cross on top of the altar.

Taos's mother and I stood together close to the altar facing our friends seated in the chapel. Nancy held Taos in her arms. He wore the white lovely christening gown that had been used by Nancy's family in the past. Present before us were the Shropshires and their boys, the Cribellis and their girls, the Rosses and their children, Tina Callaway, Russana Livermore, and the Reverend Lesley Bowers who provided the baptismal certificate. Also present were Taos's Godparents-to-be, Gloria and David Swift.

"Dear gentle, loving God," I began, "let us thank you for the special beauty and joy of this day, which is the occasion of the baptism of my son, whom I have the sacred privilege to christen in the Lord Jesus's Name."

I turned to face Taos in his mother's arms.

"My beloved son, because you were conceived in love, carried in love, and born in love, it is only fitting that your mother and I should delight in sharing this day of your baptism with a few of those friends who rejoiced at your arrival in our home and heart. Little Boy, Little Joy, today your mother and I ask our cherished neighbors, Dave and Gloria Swift, to adopt you spiritually, to pledge to love you, to stand as your Godparents before our friends here and before the eyes of God."

I then turned to Dave and Gloria who were seated on the front pew. I signalled for them to rise and come to stand beside us.

"Do you, Dave and Gloria Swift, accept this little boy, Taos, as your Godchild?"

Gloria responded, "Yes." Dave said, "We do."

Nancy then gave Taos to Gloria, who held him in her arms.

"Then as a minister in the Christian Church, and as a proud father, I baptize thee, Taos Lee Turner, in the name of the Father, the Son, and the Holy Spirit."

I sprinkled water on Taos's forehead, then dipped my thumb in the bowl and made the sign of the Cross over his little head and chest.

"Little Son, with this baptism your mother and I pledge to try to raise you as a Christian, to fill you with the love of God, in order that you may always have the strength and desire that His will be done."

I turned to those present in the chapel and asked for a brief silent prayer for Taos.

Then I turned to face Taos.

"Taos, on this day of your baptism may the Lord bless you, and may He bless those assembled here, and your Grandparents Roche and Grandmother Turner who are here in their hearts. May He bless you with physical and spiritual strength, and bring that joy into your life which comes from knowing that He loves you, and that you love Him."

Lord, I believe that in his heart, where the magic language is understood, little Taos already knows what all this means.

I pray that the day will come when he will stand before you at the Altar of your Word; and there he will aver his confirmation of his baptism, as a testimony before all.

XIII.

Lord, never have I felt more thankful than I do this day.

My wife and son and I are alive.

Yesterday, we were driving back from Texas, where we had taken Taos to see my mother. It was her first occasion to see him since he was born. Little Taos took naturally to his grandmother, and enjoyed her sweet baby-talk and being held in her arms.

I felt a pain in the core of my being as we left my mother standing on that corner lot waving us goodby. On that corner was where I sank my roots in this world. There is where my mother has lived as long as I have known her. And never once in my life have I taken leave of her without feeling this pain.

But we had a lovely sky when we drove out of Stratford and it remained with us until we came to Kit Carson where menacing dark clouds suddenly appeared on the northern horizon accompanied by vehement winds.

Beyond Limon a deluge hit us without quarter. I had to slow down in the driving, relentless rain. Nancy turned on the radio, and we heard repeated announcements that the Platte River was flooding in Denver, where many peo-

51

ple were abandoning their homes. Normally, we would drive through Denver, then take 85 north to Greeley, but there were warnings now that 85 was cut off at Fort Lupton, where the river was crossing the road.

"Doll," I said, "we'll turn north at Bennett, and take the route of Prospect Valley. That land is flat, so there can be no flooding there."—which proved to be a bungling judgment if ever one was made, since a flat country needs only a few meagre hills running beside the roads in order to flood. Now Lord, is it not a fact that we learn many of our most vital lessons in life the hard way, assuming, of course, that we are fortunate enough to survive the major errors whereby we can learn at all?

After turning off of the superhighway, we found things going quite nicely at first. I had driven this route many times, in order to make a short trip of teaching my night classes in Limon. But it is curious how often we fail to see the realities of our environment as they actually are. That flat country of a sudden turned out to be not so flat at all. Indeed, it was simply far hillier than I had ever observed it to be, and there were *waves* of water careening down their slopes forming gushing rivers on both sides of the road. Only periodically, however, did the water run across the road for brief stretches, and it appeared never to be more than four to six inches deep. We drove through several of these little ponds of water which seemed quite shallow and not more than fifty feet across. In fact, we grew so accustomed to shallow flooding that when we finally came to a deep lake on that seemingly flat road we were unable to perceive it for what it was, namely, a potential death trap of water as deep as our door latches—with enough drive to sweep us away.

Now I should have seen in my mind how deep the water was, inferring it from the fact that the guidepoles along the shoulders were inundated up to their reflectors. But that logical connection did not make itself in my head, nor was I discouraged by the fact that the water covering the road extended for more than a hundred yards. Like a fool, I did not stop and take time to study the situation; rather, I drove straight into it, deeming it just another shallow flooding which we could easily cross.

Lord, were you surprised to hear my sudden appeal to you for help when, in only seconds, I found my heart skipping beats, and found my dread going all the way back to Korea? There sat Nancy-bo beside me with Taos in her arms, I thinking, Dear God, without a miracle how can we possibly come out of this alive? And yet, I had the sense not to leave it up to you at all; or else, lost in the emotional immediacy of a pure crisis, I simply instinctively drove so as to keep the car on the road. I recall Nancy not uttering a single word, as I coped with raging waters that at any moment might thrust us into the clutches of death. In the bar-ditches the rushing water ran deeper than our car. The water climbed up to our door handles and penetrated into the floor over our shoes. At times I felt the car lift up as though it were going to be carried away. And each time it suddenly shifted sideways I felt my heart lose a beat. Yet somehow, I managed to keep it wheeled in the direction of the road, until finally we drove out of the lake onto unflooded pavement. Accompanying this strain were the sheets of rain striking the windshield so violently I sometimes lost sight of where to steer. On these occasions, I froze.

I find it odd, indeed, that no water got into our exhaust. Perhaps it is because I gradually fed more gas to the engine, to give the car more thrust. I suddenly imagined that if the pressure of the exhaust was greater than the pressure of the water, then there was no reason why, from the standpoint of that factor alone, the car should ever stall.

But then, why, with all that frenzied water under the hood, did it not drown out the motor? I have difficulty believing that the wiring and firing system was quite as waterproof as that—but apparently it was.

Lord, let me thank you for our coming out of that alive, whether you had a hand in it or not. I know that better souls than I have petitioned divine intervention which never came through. I know that misfortunes have drowned others who were far more deserving than me. Still, it seems a miracle that we plowed through that flood intact. Nancy fell into an abyss of fright. Yet she never lost her reason, nor her possession of the situation. She clung to little Taos, like guarding the divine pearl. It is interesting, and I am glad for the fact, that he did not perceive it as dangerous at all. On the contrary, he just seemed to be fascinated by it, especially the hard pounding of the rain on the car.

Shortly ahead, we came upon a huge semi-trailer stalled in the middle of the road. It had three tiers of sheep skittishly and shrilly baa-ing like mad. I parked behind it, and walked up to find its two drivers comfortably asleep in their cabin. I climbed up and opened the driver's door, and he awoke and greeted me kindly. He offered me a swig of whiskey, and said: "That lake ahead is uncrossable. So, you might as well settle in." Ahead we could see the bridge flooded over with a car sunk in the water almost up to its top. There were four men trying to push it out, who eventually succeeded even though they were working in high pressure waters up to their chests. I'm sure that this stretch of water extended several hundred feet. It took about two hours for them to push their car out, whereupon they got into it and sat into the night.

"Those fools," the truck driver said, "they should never have tried to brave that water. Now their car will be ruined, and they can't even legally sell it without declaring that it was flooded out and under."

We carried no critical supply of food. Fortunately for Taos, however, Nancy had not yet completely weaned him from suckling. He seemed contented with the two jars of baby food and her milk. At five o'clock the gushing water in the bar-ditch washed out the telephone pole beside us, which continued to hang and bob from its wires. Fearful that the wires would snap, we drove around the truck and parked in front of it, facing the lake ahead. There we sat until six o'clock that following morning, when I discovered that our right front tire was flat. The sun rose on me as I fixed it, and I watched the big truck pass around us to brave the lake. They trudged through it and then disappeared on the other side.

All night long the radio had predicted that the waters would mount. But happily, at about two o'clock in the morning they began to recede. We had been hemmed in, fearful that we might be washed away with the road. Taos slept in his little basket in the back seat. Not once did he awaken or cry. He merely made those little sounds that are natural to him in his sleep. A couple of times he snored.

At six thirty I swung the car around and drove back to the lake that had threatened our existence. It obviously had receded enough that it would not exceed our bumper. This time, I did not drive into it like a bungling fool. Rather, we studied it very thoroughly and decided that we could drive through it safely. Some of the highway markers had been washed out, but the remaining ones stood more than two feet above the water which largely had lost its force. Even so, the water covered the exhaust as we plowed through it holding our breath.

Lord, I thank you that we survived that ordeal. Who knows but what my stupidity might have killed my wife and son.

How precious life is. And on what a gossamer thread it hangs.

In the future, when I learn we are approaching a flood, I assure you we will turn around and scoot off in the opposite direction like a scared rabbit.

XIV.

Time flies like a whip of lightning.

It seems to his mother and me that little Taos has been here with us forever. Yet, we remember every day how long we searched to find him. We know how new he is to our lives, and how precious is his presence. This afternoon we celebrated his first birthday, putting one candle on his little cake.

Although he is but a toddler, the rapidity of his growth has given me an apprehensiveness about the passage of time. It seems that just yesterday I carried him in my arms as a newborn, feeling afraid that I might drop him and break him into pieces. Some of our friends are parents who have raised their children to maturity. All have counselled us nostalgically: "Hold onto him now as tight as you can, for tomorrow he will be gone." Or: "Stay as close to him as possible now, my friends, for he will soon start to get away."

Lord, it pains me to ponder that only yesterday he was born. I don't like to think that in a flash of time he will be where I am now, and I will be gone. In fact, though in a sense I feel she has been mine forever, it seems only yesterday that I met his mother. How fleeting are our lives. How brief is a day. How quick is the tide of time.

Little Taos's life has only begun. Yet, I am certain that his time will fly like mine. I recall my perception of time as a boy, how slowly the clock moved, as I sat restlessly watching it in a second grade class room, waiting for the recess bell. I remember how eternally long the school year would seem, as I began it in September, pondering the length of nine months. And what an enthralling sense of freedom when school ended in May, to last for a whole three months! But now I know for certain, Lord, that although the quality of the passage of time seems to vary according to our minds, yet it is fleeting for all, and its passage is faster than I dare to concede.

Little Taos has grown out of his earlier clothes, and we have given most of them away. Some of them his mother and I intend to keep, with a tear in our eye, to hold onto the past. We know that the past is the past; we have to live with the gone, the lost, the has been, the no more. Yet, our being is grounded in the past, and the meaning of our present existence feeds through its roots in the past.

Today at his party, little Taos received his first leather shoes. They are size infant-4½. In her trunk in Stratford, my mother still possesses the first shoes I ever wore. They are of tattered black leather, forty-seven years of age. When I am eighty-five, I too will open my trunk now and then, and pick up little Taos's original shoes with my old hands.

XV.

Taos is now sixteen months old.

He is a little dynamo, an energy factory, with an inexhaustible and indomitable will to live. He has learned to enjoy playing alone. He seems categorically an autonomous agent. And although he often is the subject of our discipline, he nonetheless obviously is the king over himself. But of course, we are the center of his life; he loves us with all of his being; and consequently, he cherishes playing with his Mommy and Daddy most of the time. Which means, by the time I return home from work each day in the afternoon, he has virtually run his mother to a frazzle, and by seven thirty in the evening he has exhausted his Daddy.

Taos's awareness of his environment, and his personal relationship with everything in it, now has reached the height of his responsiveness in life. Every moment of his existence he seeks *meaning* in the persons and objects around him, and he appears unwilling to ever settle for anything less than all the meaning that he can possibly find.

Lord, do you remember my once telling you how I was fascinated by Jesus's pithy allusion to little children as those who are greatest in the Kingdom of Heaven? I told you that I wondered what it was Jesus might have had in mind that would prompt him to put a little child above his own disciples.

I think now that I know precisely what he had in mind. I think I understand it well. And I have gotten this understanding not from reading learned essays on child psychology or morality, but simply from watching how my little son lives.

I have noted that Jesus alluded specifically to *little* children, not to older ones, since it is obvious that even as early as two years children generally begin to discover ways to behave corruptly. I have noticed in the behavior of my friends' children three years and older that already they have learned something about how to practice deception, about ways to be cruel, and about ways to hate and hurt those with whom they have conflicting interests.

Although Taos throws temper tantrums, it is obvious that he never hates his Mommy or Daddy, but merely hates the unpleasant experience of feeling frustrated in his life pursuits—which is a healthy response without which no person could ever survive in this world. Of course, his mother and I try not to reinforce his bad behavior by rewarding his attempts to get things by throwing fits. Taos is merely acting intelligently, exercising his will to get something he wants one way if he cannot get it another. I suppose this also is an essential disposition towards the world, without which no one could ever survive. However, it happens that under given circumstances there are some things we simply are not entitled to possess at all, especially if it is at the cost of needless discomfort or suffering on the part of other persons. Consequently, when little Taos throws himself on the floor and screams (unconscious that such behavior is not commensurate with his own long range needs and interests—not to mention the needs of others), we simply ignore him, or turn our backs to him, or just walk away. And this certainly has proven to be very effective, for Taos already is minimizing his number of tantrums. He is learning that this is not a successful way to accomplish his goals, or to fulfill his real life needs.

Lord, we never pleasure in seeing little Taos suffer. And unmistakably, he does sometimes suffer enormous pains of frustration when we see fit to obstruct his having his way. But we have no intention of allowing him to grow up pampered and spoiled. He must learn that no person can go through life always having his way, unable to distinguish between real life needs and mere self-centered desires. We can usually see, as sometimes Taos cannot, that he does not really need what he desires, just as he sometimes does not desire what he really needs. For example, he generally *desires* carte blanche liberty to the ice box; he desires the liberty to take anything out of it he wishes, and to spread it over the kitchen, dining room and living room floors according to any notions that strike him, just *ad arbitrium*.

Yesterday morning, Nancy-bo received a phone call from her sister Patti in Greenwich—which she took in the hallway out of sight of the broom closet and ice box. Apparently she and Patti got exuberant over some topic, since their conversation lasted for about twenty minutes. Meanwhile, Nancy thought Taos was in the kitchen doing what he generally does, i.e., making normal noises with the pots and pans (his favorite toys) and playing with the brooms. We had moved all detergents, poisons, and any other possibly toxic agents out of Taos's reach, plus any objects of any kind that he could conceivably hurt himself with or break. We once thought that we should lock up the broom closet, but decided not to, on the grounds that Taos knew how never to hurt himself with the brooms, and could never use them to damage anything because nothing was within his reach. Besides, Taos dearly loves to play with his brooms.

He can manipulate them, control them, and do things with them more than he can do with any of his common toys. Obviously, he feels that with his brooms he can have an impact on his environment, exercise his urge to creative self-expression, and fulfill his desires more than he can do with any of his factory made toys.

But that his mind is more explorative and imaginative than ours (with regard to what can be done with brooms) is now a clearly understood fact. For while his mother was on the phone, Taos took out the long broom, worked it behind the handle of the big door of the Frigidaire, and pulled it open with ease. Whereupon, he discovered a whole new kingdom of goodies, plus many exhilarating new possibilities for creative culinary adventures in the kitchen. He opened the bottom shelf filled with vegetables, took out the little carton of mini-tomatoes for salads, tore off the plastic wrapper, then proceeded to spread them over the kitchen rug. Then, he removed a bottle of salad dressing from the next to bottom shelf of the big door, pulled out its glass stopper, and with his good culinary instincts set about to pour it onto the strewn tomatoes. On top of this he aimed the broom handle at the top shelf of the ice box, dislodging one of the cartons of fresh eggs which fell to the floor at his feet. Then with his native good sense of the gourmet, he proceeded to break some of them onto the salad dressing over the tomatoes. Finally, he returned to the ice box and picked up the bowl of taco-casserole (left over from the previous evening meal), carried it into the hallway where his mother was on the phone, and presented it to her with a broad grin. It was obvious that he had already satisfied his own hunger, since his face was smeared from ear to ear.

Lord, only you know how much fun Monkeyshines must have found in doing such a thing. But surely, he was acting on an unenlightened desire, not on a real life need.

Certainly, he does have a need for adventure, creative self-expression, and to find self-fulfillment in doing whatever he is doing. But his mother did not *need* to discover that mess (for she was indeed aghast), nor need to be subjected to the uncalled-for hard work of having to clean it all up.

Yet, this little episode was not without its lesson in love.

The magic of Taos lies in the fact that *he* could do such a thing and be joyfully remembered for it (we shall never forget this); whereas, if I myself had done such a thing, my woman would begin to question my mental health, to say the least.

I need not tell you, Lord, that this incident is just one entry on the long list of "cute things" for which we shall always joyfully remember our son as a little boy.

XVI.

Frankly, Lord, before little Taos came into our lives I tended to see all children basically as nuisances and brats. I was not blind to some of the cute things they do, nor to how pretty and cherubic some of them appear. But I positively did not regard any of them as someone with whom I would care to spend much time—with the smell of their burp, their highly self-centered demeanor, and the fundamentally noisy quality of those endless meaningless nonsense syllables emanating from their mouths. In short, I felt this way because I did not see in little children the intrinsic value which they actually have within them, which Jesus could see as clearly as the sky at noon.

But now, Lord, my son has opened my eyes.

Through my love for him, and through my appreciation of the quality of his love for me, I now can see clearly the reasons for Jesus's superlative esteem for little children. By being the way he is, Taos not only charms me to love him as my son, but to love him distinctly as a little person of intrinsic beauty, which helps me to see other children who are not my own also as special persons, rather than basically as imposing little annoyances and dummies.

Now that I look at my son as he really is (which is something made possible by *love*), I see him not at all as I used to see others his age, namely, as messy, cacaphonic, and generally over-active little trouble makers who are intellectual and moral dunces; rather, I now see him as the most authentically intellectual person, genuinely moral person, and aesthetically admirable person I've ever known in my life. Now if this sounds like a naive father victimized by romantic filial prejudice; or, if it seems to smack of mockish paternal sentimentality, then Lord, life has taken me in and I am a veritable fool. But if this is the case, then I deeply lament the fact that not all men are fortunate enough also to have become such fools—and I plan to remain a fool all of the days of my life.

In his loving wisdom, Jesus saw in little children in general what I now see in Taos.

Taos has in his nature a complete disposition to *trust*. He trusts his mother and he trusts me; for he depends *in toto* on us for his well-being, his happiness, indeed his very existence. Taos would die if we neglected him. If we took leave of our home and left him locked inside it by himself, having abandoned him to the fates, then he would be helpless to save himself from dying because he is a hapless little boy. But we have shown our care and love for him in such a way as to fill his heart with an awareness of its goodness; so now, he trusts in us implicitly and verily.

Lord, isn't this precisely the kind of trust you want us to have in you?

I realize that there are children who have been cared for responsibly by no one. Many have been rejected, rebuffed, and consistently mistreated by the people who are in charge of them and by the people around them. It is understandable that such unfortunate children would learn to *dis*trust others, since they have never known the joy of personal love and responsible care. I cannot imagine how anyone could learn the meaning of your divine love and reason until first he is the beneficiary of some profound and reasonable love from some human being who cares for him on this earth. There is no reason why we should love you, Lord, if we did not benefit from your love in some way. I believe that you inspire worship because of your benevolence, Dear God, not merely because of your power. If your power were not used in benevolent ways, then you would be diabolical rather than divine, and we should have no cause to love you at all. But in our home little Taos has tasted the sweetness of careful love every day of his life. No day has passed when he has not felt the beauty and meaning of warm protection, and he always responds to it positively with what it always deserves, namely, *trust*.

Taos has nothing in his heart that would lead him to betray the goodness that he is the recipient of in the warmth of this home.

He responds to our love with love. We rejoice in his being, and in turn he rejoices in our being. It is not in his nature to respond to positive care with negative care. In the purity of his little child's heart he sees the intrinsic value of our responsible love, and he places himself entirely in its care. While of course he cannot conceptualize it verbally in his little mind, in the wisdom of his heart he knows that it is only logical and reasonable to respond to love with love. Taos has no corruption, no perversion in his nature. He cannot and will not respond to love with hate. He cares for care. He loves love. And he most appreciates those things in life that are most worthy of appreciation. He could never, and would never, appreciate being despised, abandoned, or beaten. When he reaches out to love (which evinces the spark of the divine that is inherent in his nature), he knows in his loving heart that his love should be welcomed for the intrinsic beauty that lies within it—and he trusts that he will be loved in return.

Jesus had a few absolutes in his teachings, and one of them is that love can never be forced. Heaven is love—creative, careful, responsible love. I know that "The Kingdom of Heaven can never be taken by force." Not even you, Lord, can force us to love you. It simply is not in the nature of things that love can be forced. Taos has a native rational logic in his little mind that enables him to know this perfectly. He simply would never respond to force with love.

Implicit in Jesus's teachings is the fact that we can never cure lovelessness with more lovelessness. Nor can we ever cure blind irrational hatred with more blind irrational hatred. Nor heal cynicism with more cynicism, or perversion with more perversion. Jesus taught that we can teach the value of responsible love only by responsible loving.

The hope of Christianity is that the careful heart will charm the careless heart. But it does not always succeed in doing so with adults, nor with adolescents, nor indeed always even with older children. Only *little* children can be definitely and certainly captured by love; for they are acting by their given nature, which they have inherited from you, Dear God—before they have had a chance to learn of perverse ways of behaving, which then enables them to freely choose.

Lord, who knows better than you how often we adults freely choose not to respond reasonably to reason, or lovingly to love? No sooner do we learn the *price* that we have to pay for responsible love, but what then we may freely decide that we are unwilling to pay that price.

Dear God, thank you for Jesus. He is the perfect, ultimate example of the price that the careful heart may have to pay for its care, when that very care is rejected or improperly understood.

It has been said that we are made originally in your image, Lord. And it has been said that it is in your nature to love for the sake of love. I know this now beyond the breath of a doubt. And I know it not because I have read impressive books on theology or Christology, but because I have seen demonstrative proof of it in the spirit of my little son—in whose nature your image is clearly reflected.

Taos would never respond positively to coldness, but only to warmth. Nor would he ever appreciate lovelessness, bitterness, or hostility.

In the native wisdom of his little child's heart, he would never put his trust in these things.

XVII.

Three weeks ago, Nancy-bo and Taos flew off to Florida, to vacation with her family in the balmy beauty of a little palm-lined town. With their three children and grandchildren, Jack and Marie Roche gathered in a fine home sitting on a warm beach facing the gulf breeze and sea. Every day I receive a letter from Nancy with some erratic pen marks on the envelope representing Taos's greetings and love. Some pictures show that he is growing tan; he now is fully recovered from his flu, and he and his mother build castles in the sand. Would that I were there at their side on the beach, to play race and chase on the sand. In yesterday's letter I learned that Taos has two new teeth—they seem always to come through in pairs. Because of his tan Nancy calls him Little Indian. Everyone admires his fabulous form—his broad shoulders, full chest, narrow hips and trim frame. Taos has never carried baby fat. He has never had the pot belly of a typical babe. He walks proud, erect, and straight.

Lord, how I miss my wife, my little son. I miss them like winter misses the spring, like the mocking birds miss the summer mornings. I miss the afternoon ritual of our walking together around the block. Taos loves to go off on tangents. He likes to turn onto someone's private sidewalk, and walk up to their door. No longer does he crawl up the steps. He *steps* up the steps, as a little man. But of course, we can hardly let him linger on the property of other peoples' homes, much less wander into their back yards among growling dogs—although Taos knows full well that they are confined behind big fences and can't jump on him or bite him. He has an instinctive sense of danger, however, and proceeds to retreat when they growl or bark too fiercely. Our trips around the block are rather new to Taos; they are an untold adventure which, due to his rather tiny steps, last usually at least an hour. He relishes walking around the park, throwing bread to the ducks. Once a big goose attacked him, and bit him on the cheek. I had no notion that they would hurt him, or even care to get that close to him. Taos cried traumatically. But now some days later he still loves them, although he is careful never to allow them to get too near. He marvels at the beauty of life in the park.

Most of all, I miss our evening ritual of wrestling and playing hide-and-seek. Lord, I'm sure little Jesus must have wrestled with Daddy Joseph. But neither Joseph nor little boy Jesus could ever have enjoyed it more than little Taos and I. I deeply enjoy wrestling with my little boy. Taos wrestles the way he does everything else—*with all of his being*.

He plays with all of his being. He laughs with all of his being. When he has fun, he has fun in all of his being. When he gets hurt, he cries with all of his being. Taos has learned the joy and fun of hugs and kisses. When he kisses he opens his mouth wide, like a baby sparrow opening wide its beak for its mother to drop in a worm. Autonomous as a cat, Taos decides strictly for himself when he is in the mood for exchanges of affection. If he is not in the mood for hugging and kissing, then forsooth, there will be no

70

hugging or kissing. But he does treasure these affections; he prizes the beauty and meaning of their warmth and love, and when he hugs and kisses, which I'm glad is very often, he hugs and kisses with all of his being.

I miss the Thursday mornings—my mornings for sleeping in. Taos comes into the bedroom hollering *"Da dee!"* then pulls the covers from over my shoulders. He never stops until I awake, as though he knows that he is the most lovable alarm clock Daddy ever had. We then rush headlong into a rough wrestle, and play King of the Bed. After which, he rides over Daddy's shoulders downstairs to breakfast.

Lord, my little son's laughter, when we play, is the sweetest sound on earth; it is a pristine revelation of his innocence, his joy, the creative beauty that is his life.

My little boy is my new key to understanding Jesus. And Jesus is my key to understanding your truths. Taos is living testimony to the wisdom of Jesus's teachings, to the divinity of His heart. Taos's innocence is proof that he was made in your image, blameless and pure in the nature that you gave him.

We are corrupted; we are in sin, when we do anything less than all that which you have made it possible for us to do, in the pursuit of life's meanings, beauties, and goodness. Jesus abhorred apathy and docility. He hated slovenliness and laziness. He despised lukewarmness in the pursuit of life, as I would despise my broth cooled. Bitingly he declared: "I know you well—you are neither hot nor cold; I wish you were one or the other! But since you are merely lukewarm, I will spit you out of my mouth!"

If I understand this correctly, Lord, it means that you want us to *really live*, to get out of life all of the good that you have made it possible for us to get out of it—out of every moment of all of our days. Jesus insisted that he came only to make our lives more abundant, that we be not deprived of any of the blessings which you in your bounteous generosity wish us to have. It is unmistakable in Jesus's teachings that authentic existence for a human being means seeking and receiving all that you want us to have. Our existence is inauthentic when we settle for less, when we neglect our possibilities, when we choose to live less abundantly than you have made it possible for us to live. Lord, I must confess readily that I too am caught up in sin. I have not become even half of all the good things that you have made it possible for me to be. I've never done even half of all the good things that you have made it possible for me to accomplish.

I ponder what I might be now if I had responsibly exercised my freedom to actualize all of the possibilities you have placed in my life. I compare myself as I am with the self that I could and should have become, and I shudder. Nor do I find consolation in seeing that others have fallen as far short as I. Lord, we all bungle our lives. No adult ever dies with a nice clean white slate, having done all the good things that you have made it possible for him to do. We all die failures. It surely must be just a question of extent.

Except for little children, who have never fallen short at all.

Most of us tarry in lukewarmness, whether or not we are willing to admit it. Instead of living fully (as Jesus besought us to do), we spend half of our effort trying to avoid real living. We half-work, half-learn, half-love, and even half-play. But this is not the case today, nor has it ever been, with my little son.

Taos never half-does anything. Whatever he decides to do, he does it *with all of his being*. He is never cold, and never lukewarm. He projects himself wholeheartedly into everything that he does. From every moment of his existence he tries to extract as much beauty, value, and meaning as it is possible for him to seize. He plays wholeheartedly. He loves wholeheartedly. He gives of his whole self to those whom he loves. He wholeheartedly hopes. He wholeheartedly seeks. Every morning when he awakes, he *marvels* at the fact of his existence. Then throughout all of the day he *marvels* at the reality of the things around him. He sees the intrinsic beauty informing the existence of the simplest things, which most of us older people have long ago lost our ability to see. We have become blinded, or at least partially blinded, to the beauty and goodness inherent in the miracle of the most common things surrounding us daily. But little Taos *sees* that the existence of anything at all is a miracle; he reaches out to everything to touch it, to explore it, to seize from it in every respect all of the glory inherent in the mystery of its being.

Lord, it is obvious now why Taos protests being put to bed before he is ready to literally *fall* asleep from sheer exhaustion. It is because he appreciates life, is devoted to it, and seeks to embrace its every value with the totality of his being. I lower him into his crib before he is yet asleep. And he protests, because he feels we are interfering with his right to the fullness of life. We are trying to stop him from pursuing life's meanings when he is not yet ready to stop. We are restricting his liberty to live life abundantly. And so, he *cries*.

Of all of your infinite, abounding blessings, Lord, Taos wishes not to miss a thing.

XVIII.

How can you say that children are somebody special to God," asked a confused person, "when it is obvious that they do nothing but excrete constantly from both ends, burst your ears with their deafening screaming, and tax your nerves until they simply are rubbed raw? Thank God my 'ex' got custody of mine, so that now I can restore some semblance of calm in my life. If God had to wipe their butts, clean the snot from their noses, and put up day and night with their coarse bawling, I hardly think he would put them on a pedestal simply because they aren't yet old enough, or powerful enough, to turn against him."

I will withhold judgment of this man, Lord, who has abandoned his woman and forsaken his children. You must understand, as I cannot, what the extenuating circumstances might be (if there are any at all) to explain his attitude and how it came about. Maybe his nerves *are* weaker than mine. I must admit that there have been times when Taos's behavior has put me truly on edge. His mother's nerves are made of iron. I'm sure she is able to take his squalling easier than I. Perhaps this unhappy man abandoned his family for some reasons that I cannot see. Maybe his background of personal experiences bore unusual frustrations and miseries, more than he could take and come through it clean.

At any rate, his misfortune certainly reminds me of my good fortune. The things that Taos has done to pressure my nerves could be counted only in a long story. Even so, because I have learned to see your image in him, Lord, I have learned to love his whole being, not excluding the many taxing things that he does.

Taos used to be incurably devoted to throwing our phonograph records out of their jackets, and to lifting the hood of the stereoplayer and turning it on. Finally, we had to tape it down, and to tie a strong string around all of the records to keep him from pulling them off of their shelves. Taos loved to open up the hood and grind the needle across a record when it was playing. Moreover, he was equally persistent in removing the fireplace irons from their rack, then banging them down against the coffee table glass. So as a matter of course, we had to tie them down with a strong string also. It seems ten thousand times that he pulled books down from their shelves, adamantly indisposed to learn the meaning of the word "no." As soon as he was old enough to do it, he formed a habit of dumping out the dirty diaper box on the floor. For Christmas, Nancy gave me a clay cookie jar, in the winsome shape of a little brown bear—an expensive item she once saw in a Greenwich store without money to purchase it at the time. Having the money later, she sought for months before finding another one like it—a precious thing. Taos took it from its box, which I mistakenly thought was put safely away and was tightly closed. Christmas night, he banged it against the bedstead and cracked it irreparably into many pieces.

A favorite pastime of Taos's is dropping anything into the commode that is small enough to fit in it—rolls of toilet paper, towels, shoes, and toys. One toy got lodged in the drain pipe, which we were able to extract only at considerable strain and expense. In fact, one plumber said that to extract it he would have to knock a big hole in the wall. Luckily, another plumber succeeded in hooking it on an augur, then pulled it out easily.

Occasionally, we dare to try to watch a show on the television with Taos in the same room. But he persists incorrigibly in changing the stations, or colors, or volume, or in simply closing its doors. It is indeed wearisome to teach him the meaning of the word "no." It is painful having to slap his hands hard enough to make the meaning of the word sink in. But we are doing it slowly, with no few pangs in our soul.

Taos loves to splash in the bathtub with Daddy; bathing with Daddy is fun and a joy. He is devoid of any inhibition, however, about urinating in the water anytime the urge strikes him.

These "taxing" things I love in my son. They are a part of his natural being, his adventures in the good life. If he did not do these things, he would be a psychaesthenic, a repressed and pitiable little soul. He eats beautifully in his high chair until he is full, whereupon, he likes to throw his food in all directions, especially at the cats and dog. Taos loves his little animal friends (Lady-bo, Grendel, Taz, and Little Friend). But he often torments them by pulling their hair, and by throwing the weight of his whole body on them—in innocent affection and play. He doesn't want to hurt them. He doesn't realize that they are being molested at all.

Lord, little son would not wish to hurt a living creature. He is trying to wrestle with them, as he wrestles with Daddy, but they interpret it differently, and get up and run away every time they see him coming.

XIX.

In little children, Jesus saw another trait generally missing in adult humanity, namely, an absolute emotional sincerity such as society often despises. Taos never wears a moral mask or guise. He rarely puts up a front, or pretends to be what he is not, or not to be what he is. Taos does love to tease, but only for innocent fun. He is never slippery, tricky, or wily. From one side of his soul to the other, Taos's character is genuine.

Now, Lord, I am not saying he has no cunning. Altogether the contrary, Taos is no dummy, and sometimes in an attempt to get his way he would manipulate us by putting on a scene. That is, he is not above the use of some "tear power" or "noise power," when a situation calls for it in his judgment. But I can hardly think of this as moral guile. Rather, it is obviously just the realistic use of his intelligence, i.e., the experimentation with stratagems he hopes will work while not yet having had the opportunity to learn better ways. Taos is guilty of no *moral* chicanery that is diabolical. It would do him a great injustice to accuse him of such. He knows nothing of the guileful ways older people use one another to accomplish *immoral* ends. Rather, he only knows that frustration is discomforting, and sometimes he will put on an act as an attempt to escape from it. It is my little son using his natural acumen, his native wits, in groping to find his way.

Lord, you know how double-dealing, underhanded, and Janus-faced we older human beings often are. You know perfectly well how circumventive, intriguing, and snaky we can be. You see the snares we set, our sell-outs, our bogus motives and sham acts. You know how we bamboozle, cheat, and throw dust into each other's eyes. Above all, you know how we try to hide from ourselves. You see us try to dupe others, then make fools of ourselves. You know how sometimes we are spiritual swindlers, intellectual hoaxsters, and moral wolves in sheeps' clothing.

But never is a little child such a person.

Granted, Taos's demeanor is seldom a seemly study in trained etiquette; he nonetheless is consistently free of insidious motives, of vicious designs, and of any form of humbug or ruse.

Lord, I have come to look upon all man-made social institutions, and upon at least half of the persons in them, as potential Trojan Horses. I have learned to give few adolescents, and even fewer adults, credit for the strength to stand straight and real before the face of truth. For it is evident that the social and political price of straightness is higher than most human beings are willing to pay. Most people put a premium on their social and financial solvency, Lord, and when this conflicts with your Will they do not want to look you in the eye. But this is nothing new to you, I'm sure. The prophets perceived it clearly, and Jesus took it as a matter of course. "Strait is the gate, and narrow is the way, which leadeth unto life, and *few* there be that find it."

Taos stands transparent before you, Lord, and before the world.

He is incapable of mendacity. He neither conceives of moral deception, nor ever tries to mislead a Soul. He is incapable of a sell-out. He always shows his insides outward—even when he is putting on an act. And his craftiness shows only in his need to escape frustration, or in his innocent desire to play. He is free from vulgarity, falsehoods, and putting on airs. Now it is not that he is without make-believe. For indeed, Taos's imagination runs free to enliven his world, to always make it a more enchanting place in which to live. But it is the make-believe of innocence, of trust, of the natural, creative disposition you put in him to see beauty in the world which we adults too often regard as drab.

Each day I see more clearly into the sacredness of my little boy's being. Lord, his quest for adventure is irrepressible, just as you intended for it to be. His quest for beauty is unwavering—he sees it, touches it, and feels it in *everything* around him that does not threaten him or hurt him. In the world that you created, Lord, *all things* are beautiful, which we adults, immured in our hardness, have lost much of our capacity to see.

I know that in many ways Taos is closer to the heart of reality than I, especially when I consider that I have gone through the mill of the formal schools. Sometimes the more we go to school, and the more degrees we get, and the more erudite and informed we become, the more we grow out of contact with reality and become intellectually lost. It makes me wonder about the wisdom of ever sending Taos to school at all. There seems to be little that I can do, insofar as guarantees are concerned, to insure that as he goes through this mill he will have the wherewithal to remain as authentic and real a person as he now it.

It is my understanding that the disciples were Jesus's closest friends. They evidently enjoyed his greatest trust, and substantially high esteem. Yet, Jesus adjured them seriously to become as a little child. It seems the secret of becoming a Christian involves mastering the art of acquiring the sophistication of an adult ("Be ye therefore as wise as a serpent")—with all of the knowledge of good and evil and the intelligent moral cunning that this entails—while remaining in character essentially a little child ("Be ye as harmless as a dove").

Jesus was the only human being in history who ever completely mastered this art. His life is an example of it par excellence, in the ideals he espoused, and in his implementation of them in his daily life. The sophistication of Jesus, the adult, is incomparable in history. Yet, he obviously was in his heart always a little child. This is evident in everything he did and said. The crucified God-man, hanging sad-eyed and aching on his Cross, was still the little God-boy.

As Jesus was able to see you in a little child, Lord, I am now able to see the mind and heart of Jesus in my little son. Jesus knew that all things which you have created in the world are beautiful. He knew that ugliness does not lie in *things*, but rather in situations, attitudes, and motives. Most of us either have grown ignorant of this fact as we have aged, or else we have chosen most of the time to ignore it—thus losing sight of the intrinsic presence of the Holy Ghost in all of your creation about us. We see much of the physical world as ugly; whereas in fact, the beauty of the Holy Ghost informs the existence of all physical things. Indeed, Lord, if your spirit were not present in the physical realities of the world, then why would there be any physical things at all? A cold northern blizzard can be destructive and killing, yet is it not truly majestic? An arid desert may be but hardened clay, yet is it not a glory?

Little Taos knows this in the wisdom of his uncorrupted senses. The things of beauty that older people generally take for granted, he studiously admires. He perceives the existence of each and every thing in the world around him as a *wonder*. He never recoils from things, as they are in and of themselves, but only from situations, when he senses that his well-being is threatened by certain kinds of relations with those things. Taos would see any tiger or lion as a thing of beauty, in and of itself. Also, he would see any automobile as a thing of beauty, and any baseball bat as a thing of beauty, etc., etc. But he could not, and would never, see any beauty in being attacked by a lion, or run down by an automobile, or beaten by a baseball bat.

It is obvious that Taos always gives the wonders of the world he lives in credit for being wonders. Only a pseudo-sophisticated adult or adolescent would claim that beauty exists only in the beholder's eye. Taos naturally is incapable of this kind of aesthetic egotism. He looks at a beautiful tree, and gives it credit for *being* a beautiful tree. He localizes beauty in the thing in itself, then marvels at the mystery of the power that makes its existence possible. Our adult corruption lies in our lost capacity, our indisposition, to see as wondrous all of the wonderful things in the world. In all quarters we are surrounded by wonders, yet we cannot see them, as a little child can. As verily, our own being is wonderful, which lamentably we often forget.

The innocence of my son is not a projection in his father's mind. Rather, it is only telling evidence of how blind I had grown before Taos came into the world. I know that he has seized my life with a great power. And his power over me lies in his natural goodness and beauty, which others lack because they have lost their innocence. Taos is totally free from false pride. Of course when he is frustrated, he often yelps or rends the air. When he cries without a good reason, we try not to reward such behavior in any way. But even when we discipline him out of necessity, and he does not understand the reasons why, he nonetheless is always quick to forgive. He is never cynical. He is never hypocritical. And he cannot sustain a grudge.

Contrast this with how slow we adults are to forgive, how we weigh our deeds in the balance of goods and rewards, and how often our goodness is begrudging.

Thus, Lord, it is no wonder Jesus exalted the little child.

XX.

As you know, I am not given to the use of superlative adjectives for describing life's common and ordinary effects. We live in an age that is full of language con-artists, of people who bombard us daily with exaggerated language trying to sell us the trivial and the banal as something beautiful and great. It is an age of shock, of verbal stridency, of gross sensationalism in literature, in the movies, on the stage, and in common everyday speech. I suppose this is just one of the many things in contemporary life that tend to make us generally suspicious of one another.

Albeit, I now find myself searching for uncommon adjectives to describe the most plain and usual things; and the reason for it, I'm certain, is the extraordinary effect that my wife and son have had on my life, influencing the way in which I now perceive ordinary things. Before I met Nancy, I hardly ever saw the dogs and cats in the street, although I'm sure that they were there then as commonly as they are now. The plain truth is, before I married Nancy, I was in some respects just a common Philistine; for obviously, much of her greater sensitivity and awareness has rubbed off on me, which is evident in the fact that I see many common things in life that I never saw before. Or to be more accurate, I always did see them, but was unable to see the richness of meaning and value that was actually inherent within them. For example, when there is a dog or cat in the street, Nancy never fails to *see* it as a living being of intrinsic value, in need of some attention and affection; for invariably, she attempts to entice the little animal to come to her, then pets it and speaks softly and lovingly to it, to bring a little more joy and meaning into its life than otherwise it would experience.

Now, I am not confessing to being a Philistine through and through, or a brute. For I have always seen in any sunset the creative magic of a Divine Artist. Certainly, one need not be an aesthete to find some flaws in human works of art. But a sunset which is painted by you, Lord, never contains a single imperfection—any more than does a fjord, or a mountain, or a tree. But before Nancy and Taos came into my life, I was blind to the fact that this is equally true of a clod of dirt, or a weed, or any common thing which has the touch of your hand upon it. Actually, I used to think of myself as someone above the plebeian soul, as someone more sensitive than normal in my assessment of the values of the good life. After all, I was raised by a mother with a matchless sensitivity to the beauties of nature that you created, Lord—not to mention her inimitable feeling for the joy of love. At least I did have the sensitivity to recognize superior sensitivity when I was in the presence of it—I married Nancy-bo, and I have felt my life be changed unbelievably by the superior spirituality of the little son she bore me.

I have discovered from Taos that, unbeknownst to me before he entered my life, my faculties of appreciation actually had grown rather dull. I certainly am not willing to attribute this to any degeneration of my will to live. My urge to live received incomparable nourishment and encouragement in childhood, and since then it has not diminished one whit. Rather, I attribute it unmistakably to the deadening effect on the human spirit of becoming caught up in the *abstractions* of the academic life, which tends to dull a man's senses to the meaning and value informing the reality of the concrete objects around him. Thanks to the daily reminders of Taos, I can now remember how as a little boy I could see infinite beauty in a rock, a fallen branch, a pile of mud. I could marvel at a stick of wood, seen ordinarily by adults as just another piece of trash to be burned or thrown away.

Now Lord, my *vision* has been restored.

Once again, I have grown intoxicated; I have laid hold of the ecstasy, I have felt my passion for life revived. In a grain of dirt, I can see the rapture of your Holy Spirit. I can see it in an "ugly" desert lizard or in a common housefly. Once I saw a fly enter the kitchen and land in sight of Taos's eyes. Its beauty, its fantastic ability to fly, excited wonder in him, as I could tell by the expression on his face and the gleam in his eye. Taos marveled at its strangeness, at the remarkable nature of this little creature. He saw it as a *living being*, pursuing its life interests to and fro. I'm sorry that I had to kill it, for it was truly another one of your beautiful creatures, Lord, simply seeking to fulfill its own needs, as I myself do everyday.

I used to believe that you wanted us to enjoy a communion with *you*, Lord. Then as I became morally more sensitive, I decided that you also want us to enjoy a communion with all of the persons around us. But now, thanks to Taos, I have regained a knowledge of what I felt intuitively in my childhood—that you mean us to enjoy a communion with the *whole of reality*.

With the earth. With all the plant life on it. With all the creatures on it and above it. And with all of the things that we touch and are touched by.

XXI.

Thank you, Lord, that my wife and son are again safe at home.

It is fantastic how little Taos grew in only three weeks. There certainly is no babe left in him. He is truly a little boy, taller, more defined in his features, and with numerous new skills. For example, when he left home he had to hold his drinking cup with both hands. Now he handles it easily and skillfully with only one hand. He has some new words in his vocabulary, in fact dozens, if we take into consideration all of his articulations that are not in the formal English heritage.

It is curious that he did not recognize me when I met him at the terminal in Denver. Nancy's theory is that it is not a question of having forgotten me—for he definitely had not forgotten anything or anyone else. Upon arriving home, he knew immediately where to go to find his toybox; he recognized Lady-bo, and all of the cats. He knew exactly where to go to find his brooms, in the closet. And he recognized all of his little peers. So apparently, he was simply *refusing* to recognize me, thinking that I had abandoned him, since after all, it had been three whole weeks since I had appeared in his life to love him and play with him (which in his little child's perception of time was a long period indeed). I'm glad that within a couple of days he completely forgave me, and that now our relations are normal. Strangely, the night before he returned home I dreamt that he would not recognize me at all.

The trip to Florida was uniquely beneficial for Taos. He is an only child, not accustomed to having to give and take much in relations with other children. In Naples, he had to play every day with seven cousins, ranging from little Jay (his own age) to Norm, who is in the second grade. At first he was withdrawn and frightened, and clung to his mother. All the other children knew each other, and were used to playing together aggressively. Taos of course did not know this, and was simply rather overwhelmed by the naturalness of their manners in play, which is not natural in the only child's life at all. Even so, Taos is essentially a very secure little boy, with a very deep self-confidence that has come naturally to him from being protected and loved. Consequently, he needed only a couple of days to acclimatize himself to the spree of their play. Taos lives for the good life. He is not one to stand back from any chance of merrymaking and frolic. In the beginning, he ventured forth cautiously. But then, he entered the romp and caper— so much so, in fact, that he made himself a nuisance to the older children. For he wanted to play with them all of the time, which they did not. The give and take was a good lesson in his life. My little son, you cannot always have what you want.

When he smiles and laughs, Taos's nose krinkles now more than ever. Lord, his little laughs have an uncanny power over me, such as I could never have imagined. There is a ring of freedom of spirit, of grace, of mirth in them that is divine.

In my daily work, I am out in the rat race, Lord. It is a catharsis of spirit to come home, to be with Nancy and Taos. The sound of Nancy's "I love you, Hubby Mine"—

is a balm. The sound of Taos's laughter is so sweet, it is a rapture.

We have a new little ritual now, on warm days. Nancy knows when I am returning home from school at noon. She brings little Taos out onto the sidewalk, where he can see me coming, and then he starts running to me, holding up his arms, hollering "*Da dee!*"

Lord, this means more to me than all the imaginable rewards of power and glory.

How can I ever thank you for such blessings?

My little boy has brought me closer to you, just as his mother's love makes me more certain than ever of the reality of your love.

How can one thank you for a fortune so great that it exceeds all understanding? How do I, a finite soul, thank you for blessings whose richness is infinite?

I stop in solitude to ponder it all, and I am stunned. I am stricken in awe. How does one thank you for the treasure at the bottom of the rainbow? For inexhaustible riches so beautiful that nothing can still their aching?

XXII.

In time, little Taos will become of age.

One September morning he will start to school. Between now and then he will learn to believe in Santa Claus. And then one day, they will try to tell him that Santa Claus is a myth. The very thought of it will hurt his heart, and he will come to his mother and me, supplicating for some reassurance that Santa Claus is real. Lord, I promise you, that we will not let his understanding of the reality of Santa be undermined. We shall proceed simply by showing him in truth what Santa really is, namely, the beauty and goodness of unselfish giving for the sake of the joy of others. I pray, Lord, that before we have finished explaining this to Taos, he will know that as long as this spirit of giving is real, Santa Claus is real, which nobody can deny, and then he will believe more than ever.

May he also learn to believe in the Great Pumpkin, the Little People, and to clap for Tinker Bell.

May he believe in you too, Lord, as naturally as though there were never such a thing in this world as disbelief. May he learn to love you, to see the beauties of nature as your handiwork, to say a prayer of thanks at each meal, and every night before he goes to sleep.

Already, Taos believes in *forever*.

In every cell in his body, to the boundaries of his soul, he believes with all of his being in the inherent goodness, the earnestness, the permanent value of life. Taos's faith in the sacred value of life knows not the corruption of a single degree of doubt. Of course, he does not formulate verbally in his little mind a concept of an immortal soul. But in his natural goodness he *takes for granted* the intrinsic value of life, and knows that its beauties and meanings should be permanently conserved. *Faith* is as natural to him as breathing and eating.

Lord, his mother and I promise to nourish this faith with daily, unceasing, inerrant love. We pray that loving you will become as natural in his life as loving us. As I was raised in the bosom of faith (on my mother's lap), so shall he be raised. In and through our love may he discover the reality and goodness of your beauty in the world. The joy of your love is something that we shall convey to him through the joy of our own love, night and day. Lord, may he come to know your love as an eternal oasis in his heart, as the enduring reliance, the bread of life.

As Taos grows, may his love for you grow. In time, we shall try to instill in him all that my mother instilled in me—an awareness of beauties so beautiful, of love so loveful, that he can never escape from inheriting its aching. It is obvious already, Lord, that in his little child's consummate faith he sees nothing less than infinite and eternal importance in his mother's and father's love. Naturally, he does not say it with words, but he *feels* it throughout the whole country of his being.

As the years pass, he will discover the meaning of freedom, of temptation, of eating of the fruit of the tree of knowledge of good and evil. Whatever evil things he might choose to do, we shall never, never cease to love him. He will always be our little boy.

Our prayer for Taos is that we can give him all of the strength that he needs through insightful love. Help us to enkindle in him that abiding light, which no heartbreak, no suffering, can ever put out. Let us love him, Lord, with such astuteness and care that his little child's faith will become a man's faith. Let us show him such a depth of love that he can never abandon its meaning, even if the storms of life tear up his body and smash him down. Let us care for him with responsible reason, in order that he can peg his dignity, integrity, and identity on responsible reason. Help us to stand as a mirror before him, that he may come to see clearly what he is, and see plainly what he can and ought to become. Help us give him the essential moral tools of life, that he may weather all of its trappings and vicissitudes with his affirmation intact. Let our guidance be a buttress to him, so that wherever he goes and whatever he does, he will know that he is loved by his mother and father who will never forsake him. And by you, Dear God, who are always in the most trying times his sustenance and his shield.

Let us give him the mortar to cement his faith, that it may weather all the winds of woe.

Lord, I would not trade my little boy for all of the money in all of the world's banks. Nor would I trade his mother for all of the power in Moscow and Washington. I not only need them now; I need them forever, for we cannot, and will never, settle for anything less than forever. I know that Jesus demands more of us than any church or formal religion does, but he also promises more, which is what makes his life and teachings valid. If we will cooperate with you intelligently, I know you can provide a way to permanently conserve the values of our love. If we will be-lieve and work, then we can go and go, throughout an endless duration of time, never reaching an end to the possibilities of what we can become, accomplish, and possess together. We can discover more beautiful beauties, more meaningful meanings, and more valuable values.

Provided, we remain always a little child.

Thank you, little Krinkle Nose, for turning my eyes back to the Kingdom.

I pray that when your mother and I are gone and you have become an old man, you will still be in your heart a little boy.

Now, you run and play. I pray that, when you are too old to walk, you will still clap for Tinker Bell.